# STICKMAKING

## Leo Gowan

The Crowood Press

# STICKMAKING

First published in 1997 by
The Crowood Press Ltd
Ramsbury, Marlborough
Wiltshire SN8 2HR

**British Library Cataloguing in Publication Data**

A catalogue record for this book is available from the British Library.

ISBN 1 86126 098 9

**Acknowledgements**
My thanks to all the many stickmakers – most of them friendly –
who have contributed (sometimes unknowingly) to the creation
of this book.

Photographs by Bill Canning, Frank Day, Eric Dixon,
Ken Hunter, John Keeling, Les Pattison, Andy Robson,
Brian Thomas, Bill Trobe, Frank Walton and Brian Wishart.

The sticks shown in this book were made by the author and
by the above photographers.

Line drawings by Andrew Green and John Worrall.

Typeset by Phoenix Typesetting, Ilkley, West Yorkshire

Printed and bound in Hong Kong by the Paramount Printing Company Ltd.

# Contents

|  | Introduction | 7 |
| 1 | Getting Started – Tools and Tackle | 9 |
| 2 | Shanks | 14 |
| 3 | Types of Stick. All-Wood Sticks | 23 |
| 4 | Deer Antler | 44 |
| 5 | Horn | 59 |
| 6 | Making Ram's Horn Handles. Crook; Market Stick; Leg Crook; Ramscurl | 69 |
| 7 | Microwave Use in Hornwork | 77 |
| 8 | The Half Stick | 81 |
| 9 | Fancy Sticks | 84 |
| 10 | The Leaping Trout | 91 |
| 11 | Horn Thumbsticks | 95 |
| 12 | Colouring Ram's Horn | 101 |
| 13 | Other Types of Handle Material. Resin; Tufnol; Deer Foot | 105 |
| 14 | Jointing and Finish | 111 |
|  | Appendix | 114 |
|  | Useful Addresses | 117 |
|  | Further Reading | 119 |
|  | Index | 121 |

## Dedication

This book is dedicated to Leonard Parkin.
His creations – our aspirations

# Introduction

Stickmaking was originally a truly rural craft with exponents countrywide from the West Country and Wales up to the Scottish Highlands and Islands. The lore concerning the craft has been handed down by generations of countrymen like the unwritten sagas of illiterate peoples.

However, with an increasing amount of leisure time and a general resurgence of interest in craft work, stickmaking is attracting more devotees from all walks of life. There are now a growing number of enthusiasts with industrial and other trade skills bringing their expertise to bear on the problems always attendant upon the craft, particularly in horn work. Older methods traditionally practised are gradually being replaced by new or refined ones, and the craft is continuously evolving with fresh ideas, procedures, and occasionally tools, apparatus and materials introduced intermittently.

The craft moreover is basically a simple one and lack of experience can be made up for in practice, patience, improvisation and enterprise. The novice, in fact, unhampered by any preconceived ideas, can often produce excellent results after a short period, comparing favourably with sticks made by those with a much longer acquaintance with the craft, whose work often tends to become rather stereotyped as a result.

Wood, antler, horn or man-made, the range of materials used is considerable, and most are readily available. Whatever the results, functional or fancy, useful or purely ornamental, plain or ornate, satisfaction is assured.

This book is a comprehensive introduction to the craft.

# 1 Getting Started – Tools and Tackle

The neophyte stickmaker need not be deterred by a paucity of tools. It is possible to start up with minimal equipment and augment this as one goes along. There is no shortage of choice nowadays, both new and used, and bear in mind that in many cases older hand tools were of much better quality than their modern counterparts. Additions are usually made depending upon the particular requirements of the type of stick one intends to create, although quite often one succumbs to the stickmaker's syndrome – acute acquisition of yet more tools.

For cutting shanks you need a folding pruning saw. This is an essential. A knife, however sharp, is fairly useless for stick cutting (although useful for trimming). You will never obtain a clean through cut and quite often access to the part you wish to cut is awkward. The pruning saw has a

*Tools and tackle in regular use.*

fairly thin tapering stainless or rust-resistant blade complete with a lock which prevents closing accidentally on your fingers. Most are Japanese, and like all of their saw-edge tools, cuts on the pull stroke. They usually have replaceable blades but literally hundreds of shanks can be cut before blunting. They are as a rule compact enough to fit into a jacket pocket. If the handle is black or brown the saw can be difficult to see at times if laid down. Put a dab of white or blue paint on to make it more conspicuous. Don't bother fitting a lanyard or loop of twine as usually these persist in snagging on twigs, brambles, and so on and are far more trouble than they are worth. A small lightweight pair of secateurs is handy for snipping off side shoots or thorns along the shank or a good sharp pocket knife would suffice. The teeth on the pruning saw blade are usually too coarse to cut smaller diameter growth cleanly without snagging.

In the workplace, whether shed, garage, loft, cellar or wherever, start with as stout a bench as possible and as large a vice as is practicable for the space available. Ideally two vices are required, an engineer's or bench type, and a carpenter's. If space or finances dictate one only I would settle for the former, with 5-inch (12.5cm) or 6-inch (15cm) jaws, as having greater versatility, particularly with regard to horn work (the foldaway Workmate type folding table with split adjustable halves of the work surface, forming a type of vice is handy for holding and perhaps straightening shanks but useless for most other stickmaking work, particularly if any leverage is required). Owing to the recession and the loss of major industries there are many thousands of engineer's vices in circulation around the country and they can be acquired quite cheaply set against new price. Try not to get a quick-release model; they have a nasty habit of going wrong fairly regularly and are extremely tricky to repair.

*A corner of the workshop. Roof glazing makes the interior much lighter than the norm.*

Also in the essential category are rasps and files. Surforms have been good performers over the years with the only drawback being that the (replaceable) blade is inclined to be rather brittle and one careless stroke can result in shattering. Spare blades are quite expensive. Wood rasps come in all shapes and sizes – and prices – but I have found that they seldom retain their cutting edges for any length of time on horn. Neither can they be sharpened of course. Several types too have the annoying tendency to clog up in use and the teeth require cleaning with a brass wire brush periodically. Better by far than wood rasps are engineering files. These are available over the counter at any engineer's supplier and are known as milled tooth files. They look more like rasps than files and are classified as Dreadnought which have curved teeth, and Millenicut with straight teeth. These are ideal tools for the shaping up of horn and either tooth pattern performs equally as well. Teeth are very sharp and it is advisable to tape about 2in (5cm) at the opposite end to the handle. You need to fit your own handle and *never* use without one. 8in (20cm) or 10in (25cm) lengths are the most useful in general but shorter and finer blades are also handy. Both will give

rapid removal of rough horn or wood, together with a reasonable finish. In fact with practice you will find that, as with Surforms, you can achieve quite a fine finish as you give them more use and become more familiar with their full capabilities. They are available both in flat and half round shapes, and have a long life without blunting.

I have never owned a bandsaw, neither can I conceive of one as being essential in the craft. A very useful tool with a good sturdy blade is a carpenter's bow saw with its facility for cutting curves, but finding a supplier of spare blades may be a problem as the tool has virtually been replaced by the bandsaw. I used tenon saws for years for general straight cutting but they blunt very quickly on horn, and the cost of professional sharpening is prohibitive. Nowadays I use a 12-inch (30cm) hacksaw. The blades are replaceable of course and fairly cheap but buy best quality as they have a much longer life. They are equally useful for either wood or horn cutting and my frame can be adjusted simply to cut at a 45 degree angle which can be handy now and again. Adjust blade tension fairly tightly as otherwise the cut tends to whiffle a bit especially in thicker material. A good, fairly coarse blade would have 18 teeth per 25mm (1in) and a finer cut 25 teeth.

A coping saw is a useful tool on occasion but the thin, flexible blade is not particularly strong and will shatter easily if it snags, as it tends to do when changing the direction of the cut. It will also overheat easily on hard wood or horn or if too deep a cut is attempted. Don't use the tool with a stop/start action, keep it moving and the blade will last much longer. If you fancy carving your handles, a good sharp pocket knife or two can often suffice but if you are really enthusiastic you will no doubt consider investing in carving chisels and gouges. Don't purchase a set of these tools; you will find that if you had, say, a collection of ten or more different types you would nonetheless favour almost exclusively only two or three for most projects. And in using any edged tool bear in mind the old saying, 'Never put in front of the blade anything that you don't intend to cut.'

Rifflers are small wood files or rasps and are useful for getting at difficult-to-reach sections of fancy work. They usually come with slightly curved ends and in different shapes; round and half-round; triangular, and so on. They are double-ended, being held in the middle and in effect you are getting two for the price of one. They can leave quite a well-scratched area after working but this can be cleaned up by rolling a piece of fine 'wet and dry' abrasive around one end and using that to smooth down. Needle files come in various shapes and either in walleted sets or individually. They are much finer cutting than rifflers and clog rather quickly, although easily cleaned with a brass wire brush. I make handles for mine with either suitable lengths of seasoned

blackthorn or holly or narrow sections of antler. They are ideal for fine horn or antler work but one or two strokes will usually result in clogging with wood. There is no need to purchase best quality as the cheapest 'street market type' last quite well and are easily replaced.

There is no doubt that it is a perfectly feasible proposition to make excellent sticks without the use of any power tools whatsoever. But it will be hard work, and very time consuming. Neither will the results be superior. I know many stickmakers throughout the country but I have never met or heard of one who claims his work to be accomplished entirely by hand. The electric drill is commonly used of course and a good range of accessories can be fitted. There is no need for variable speed or hammer action, the simplest model will do, and of choice try to obtain a lightweight model. I use a spare one permanently clamped near to one end of the workbench and fitted with a coarse grit fibre-backed sanding disc; this is in regular use as a grinder and indeed rough shaper. Flap wheels make short – and neat – work on inside curves, and flat bit or spade drills are essential when drilling handles to accept dowelled shanks. The paint stripper or hot-air gun, or even a vari-speed hair dryer is much better for heating horn than the old fashioned method of blow lamp or even (primitively and rather dangerously) holding over the top of an oil lamp funnel or meths burner.

Many stickmakers have made good use of the power file since it came on the market several years ago. The 13mm sanding belt, passing around pulleys on an arm, can certainly be a considerable asset in shaping, particularly on inside curves or sanding down; roughing out, and so on. But there are drawbacks – the sanding belts are very expensive for what they comprise and will snap with monotonous regularity, quite often after little use. When they do break the spring-tensioned arm, which has no retaining device, is projected from the machine and you can find yourself scrabbling on the floor amongst the sawdust and shavings trying to locate the spring. The dust extraction system is none too efficient, and if sanding down metal you are warned to remove the dust bag otherwise the machine may catch fire!

I quite like the tool nonetheless. Use 40 or 60 grit sanding belts rather than 120 which tend to clog and don't last long. The types recommended for use on ceramics are better than those for wood, particularly when horn or antler is involved.

Miniature power tools are tailor-made for fine detailed carving work, but if you can shape up to your satisfaction using other methods it would be difficult perhaps to justify the expenditure. A flexi shaft would be an essential for best results but can increase the outlay considerably. So too would a selection of drills, burrs, cutters, and so on. Excellent used burrs and drills can be had generally for the asking, however, from your dentist or you could purchase direct from dental supply outlets, although normally sold in batches of six or ten. Care too must be exercised in their use, particularly with horn, to ensure that overheating of the machine does not occur. Miniature power tools, generally, are not designed for prolonged use.

Another tool for fancy sticks is the woodburner or pyrography machine. Basically this is a refinement of the electric soldering iron. There are two different types; one has a variety of different shaped bits – straight cutting edge; half moon; point, and so on. These bits are not cheap

and their wiring tends to burn out, rendering them inoperative. The alternative is called the 'hot-wire' system, which is simply a wire loop (that can be shaped in various ways) connected to terminals. The wire breaks or burns out eventually of course but is easily and cheaply replaced. This system is by far the more flexible in fine work of the fur, fin or feather type and produces first-class results in wood or antler. Using either machine on horn, the outline is rather softer as the heat melts the horn where the bit or wire is in contact. Consequently a light touch is required. Light sanding down is required after using each system to remove singe or scorch marks, and any texturing can be emphasized by use of inks or other methods of colouring which will lodge in the burnt-in markings.

You will be sanding down in stickmaking on a regular basis and need to stock up on abrasives. Avoid paper-backed types (apart from the really fine grades of 'wet and dry') and try to obtain cloth- or fibre-backed whether in sheets or in discs; they are much more robust with a considerably longer life. A tool steel scraper, properly used, will remove scratches quickly but as it leaves 'flats' sanding down is needed afterwards. Even broken glass has its devotees for scraping down but I have never been tempted to adopt this system, whatever the results. Use abrasives wrapped around a cork or rubber block; these will not only apply more pressure but will do so evenly and not groove the sanded area. Alternatively make up sanding blocks rather than holding the abrasives in place by hand. Stretch a layer of rubber (Sorbo is ideal) between the block and abrasive and tack in place at the sides. Round ones can also be made using a length of dowel or offcut of shank in place of the block. For finer inside curves wrap the abrasive around a thin dog chew or a short length of reasonably firm nylon tubing such as a car windscreen wiper connection. Strapping – strips of emery cloth ½in–1in (1.25–2.5cm) wide – is often used for inside curves but unless ridden slightly sideways in use, in addition to the usual pull to and fro, will often create grooves.

Shank bark is often coarse and requires smoothing down before finishing. For this, use steel wool, coarse grade – the finer type shreds too easily and is ineffective on really crusty bark. Don't use emery or sandpaper (apart from on knots) as the finer grades will clog up quickly and coarser ones scratch the bark. Don't apply too much pressure using steel wool or that too will make scratches.

Other tools and tackle for special purposes are detailed in various other chapters.

In any workshop it is essential to have good light in the working area. A workbench by a window is an obvious situation but will not receive anywhere near as much light as when there is a roof light. I let into my workshop roof two 4ft × 2ft (1.2m × 0.6m) sections of Twinwall polycarbonate sheet and the increase in light is tremendous. Roof glazing of course gives far greater light transmission than vertical glazing of the same dimensions. Twinwall has other advantages too: it is anti-condensation coated; diffuses strong sunlight; provides much better insulation than glass and is claimed to be 200 times stronger. For darker corners a flexi neck table lamp fitted with either base or a cramp for shelf fixing is ideal for situating over the work in hand. The worst lighting of the lot is a badly situated light source behind your head where you seem to be working in permanent shadow.

# 2 Shanks

*Pruning saw, knife and secateurs with bundle of typical shanks including root ash, holly, white hazel and hazel 'twisty'.*

You can of course buy ready-to-use shanks, and being straightened and seasoned, varnished and ferruled, they have an obvious attraction although as a rule choice is limited to hazel and occasionally blackthorn. The satisfaction gained from cutting one's own is absent of course, and cost must be considered, although this is relatively slight when set against a stick which can quite often have a useful life of upwards of twenty years. Another consideration too with 'shop shanks' is their place of origin. Almost certainly they will have been coppice-grown for the trade down South or in the West Country. A hazel grown, say, in Hampshire or Somerset, on good loam and in a favourable climate, will naturally make much quicker growth than its counterpart in the thin stony soil of the Yorkshire Dales, or parts of the Lake District or the Highlands. You will rarely, if ever, be able to cut a decent diameter 4ft (1.2m) shank in the North or in Scotland with less than five or six years' growth. A Southern one would make similar growth in four years and when seasoned would be considerably lighter in weight. I find personally that the balance of a light-weight shank feels wrong especially when fitted with a horn handle which can often outweigh it by several ounces. The strength too could be suspect and I would not care to use one as a hill stick which is longer than normal to maintain one's balance when contouring around steep slopes. Nor would I trust one as a fisherman's wading pole especially in some fast flowing river where your very life could depend upon its sturdiness. In the countryside shanks abound – in field hedges, thickets and woods, disused quarries and railway embankments, canal and river banks, roadsides (including motorway embankments!); even in sheltered combes, dingles and small valleys and glens reaching way up into the hills. In urban areas many grow in parks, church-yards and often in private gardens. It's always worthwhile looking at any wood-lands where there are electricity wires overhead. They trim back any tree or shrub growth underneath the wires every five years or so and if you get there just before trimming is due you can often find nice stands of shanks growing from pollarded stumps. Pollarding of course usually results in straighter shank growth than when grown naturally. Other good sites are often near the edges of conifer planta-tions, where the dense stands of timber haven't killed off all the growth under-neath. You can often find good holly and blackthorn in such sites and on occasion others that you don't often get in decent shank lengths such as cherry and moun-tain ash. It might be productive, too, to stop and pass the time of day with anyone cutting and laying an old hedge, although you may well find that any good growths are retained by the hedger as he is a stick-maker himself!

Wherever you find them, the shanks all belong to someone, so obtain permission to cut initially – you will find that the present of a stick generally makes an offer that they can't refuse.

If a shank is growing straight out of the ground never cut it off as it stands; scrape away around the base and you may find a root (or sucker) growth attached which could provide a nice handle. Similarly if the shank comes away in a curve from the trunk or branch before straightening up try to sever it to include this curved section; this can often be jointed to a suit-able piece of horn or antler to provide a most attractive – and serviceable – hand-piece.

Aim for a cut length of 4ft (1.2m) or so on average, but naturally cut longer or shorter according to availability. The shorter ones can be elongated using a longer-necked handle whilst the longer ones give a greater choice of diameter. If you want, say, a diameter of 1in (2.5cm) at the handle end of the eventual chosen length cut the shanks rather larger than that. Planked timber shrinks on average between 10 per cent–15 per cent during seasoning and sticks naturally do likewise. Remember too that this shrinkage is in the diameter and not the length. This will save you exasperation when you inspect a bundle of last year's shanks and wonder what on earth possessed you at the time to cut some of those thin ones! Bends can be put right easily enough so don't be too concerned if all shanks cut are not straight. Cutting a straight shank doesn't neces-sarily result in a straight seasoned one; you will often be faced with bends that you could swear were not there originally. Any shank can have some thicker or stronger fibres that will contract when seasoning more slowly than others but will exert a stronger pull when they do. Conversely, some thinner fibres will season more quickly than others and this contraction can put a bend in a straight shank. Distortion can also occur when one side of a bundle is exposed to sunlight (thus heat) more than the rest, or be in a draught which will hasten seasoning on that side. Avoid shanks with kinks; you can never straighten them satisfactorily and you often end up with an unsightly knuckle. Good shanks abound and you can hardly be so desperate that you need to cut one with a kink.

The accepted wisdom regarding the best time to cut shanks has always been that the winter months are best, the sap being dormant then. Nonetheless for years I have nearly always cut some during summer holidays and have found that all have seasoned without any problems. Nowadays I cut virtually at any time during the year, the chief problem being that foliage density makes seeing them problematical during the summer.

All shanks need to be seasoned before use and the long-held belief has always been that this period should be at least a year (although I have heard two and even three years quoted on occasion). For a few years now however I have experimented with the seasoning period and find that shanks in general need no longer than eight or nine months, although the close grain of holly and blackthorn will extend that period up to about a year.

Make up your shanks in bundles of a dozen or more and tie tightly near top, middle and bottom. Use cord or twine soft and thick enough not to dent the bark. Label to show date of cutting. The ties will ease to a certain extent during seasoning and if you don't have too many bundles you can tighten if you wish. This is not really essential however as it will have little influence on the eventual straightness of the shanks for reasons already quoted.

I store mine in a garden shed and also a garage but a porch or any spare room would do provided that it is not heated. A lean-to against a wall or shed is adequate, or a car-port; even a makeshift frame with roof providing protection from rain. It doesn't matter if they are propped up or lying flat but don't stretch across rafters or sleepers or they will bow. They can rest on wood, concrete or gravel, but not soil. Beware of woodworm if stored in a shed, although creosoted walls and floor act as a deterrent. Alternatively stand them in a

bucket with a few inches of paraffin for twenty-four hours, then reverse for another day before storing.

# BEST SHANK WOODS

The 'Big Four' in stickmaking are ash, blackthorn, hazel and holly.

## Ash

It is said of ash that it will survive in many places but thrive in only a few. It is intolerant of shade, unlike hazel, and demands rich moist soil if it is to make quick growth. In poor conditions most shanks found will taper too quickly to be worth cutting, unless one is requiring 3ft (1m) lengths only. Rarely will you find decent 4ft (1.2m) lengths in these situations. The bark is rather coarse and will usually be well-studded with knots where shoots have been removed. Greyish in colour, lightly tinged with a green undercast, it is not particularly attractive. You can spend a productive few minutes however after seasoning in rubbing down with coarse steel wool and transform the appearance considerably. Buff down to the underbark which is a nice shade of green and quite smooth. It will also be mottled or flecked with grey from the outer bark but don't remove these as they enhance the appearance. The green will fade with age to a grey-brown shade which is quite pleasant but isn't show-winning standard. If you cut fairly thick shanks ash is a good subject for bark stripping and with regular rubbing down with linseed oil turns out a very pleasing honey-coloured shade with a prominent watermark effect in the wood. The bark and underbark are quite thick so you need a good diameter shank initially. Don't debark until the shanks are seasoned.

Shanks will not usually be as straight as hazel, with many bends tending to start from where side shoots sprang, but straightening does not present any great problems. Ash is a strong and flexible wood used in furniture-making and for tool handles and is ideally suited for stick-making, but don't expect to make show sticks from it. Sand down knots flush; they look better that way rather than standing proud.

## Blackthorn

It is much easier to find blackthorn growing than it is to find a good black-thorn shank. The bushes can be seen at a good distance in early spring when they produce snow-white blossom before the leaves appear. It is an extremely spiny wood and the shoots and branches as a rule are all tangled together with little straight growth. Fortunately it can be found reasonably straight if in a hedge which is trimmed regularly – but not at intervals of less than five years! It also throws out horizontal root growth which produces suckers. These grow fairly straight normally and are not so thorny as branch growth although tending to become spinier with age. The bark varies from a very handsome deep rich shade of reddish mahogany to lighter shades, sometimes tinged with silver.

You will need good thornproof gloves when cutting blackthorn (hedger's gloves, from farm supply stores, are best) and also pruners for trimming the spines. It is often necessary to trim *in situ* as the shank may not budge otherwise! I usually carry, if the site is not too inconveniently situ-

ated, a pair of long-handled shears to sever the top of the shank whilst still in the bush to facilitate pulling it clear. If you have any distance to go don't be too ambitious with the number of shanks that you can carry; blackthorn is a very close-grained wood and heavy. It is particularly prone to splitting along the cut edges so seal the ends as soon as possible. I have found after trying various methods over the years that the best end sealer is horticultural grafting wax (from garden centres, and so on). Melt slightly using a hot-air gun or hair dryer and brush on. A suitable 'brush' can be made from a short length of (preferably) natural fibre – such as hemp – rope with the cut portion teased out and bound about an inch or so back from the end.

Although this is possibly the most attractive of all stickmaking woods the weight means that a popular stick size of a 4ft (1.2m) length makes quite an unwieldy proposition if you have been accustomed to, say, a lighter hazel. However it is ideally suited for a shorter sturdy type of stick, and also much easier to find in these shorter straight lengths. You will when cutting see many that are beautifully straight up to about 3ft (1m) or so then for no obvious reason form a dog leg, or taper quickly.

Blackthorn polishes beautifully and looks far more impressive with the knots left standing proud. Many shanks when cut will be found to have an oval cross-section. This is not a drawback and indeed can be a bonus as antler, for instance, when trimmed to handle size is often similarly shaped. It is not much of a problem to fit other types of handles either for that matter, and an oval handle grip is just as comfortable as a round one. Do not be tempted to stain the bark black as I have seen frequently. It ruins the looks of a stick which has probably the most beautiful of all bark.

## Hazel

This is the universal favourite. Indeed as a shank it can hardly be faulted and it is reasonably widespread throughout the greater part of the country, except certain areas of upland Wales and Scotland. It grows fairly straight with a decent taper as a rule, and is almost certainly used in the making of at least 90 per cent of all sticks made in Britain. Bends present no problems in straightening.

More than any other shank wood it has by far the greatest bark colour variations and indeed can be plain or mottled. There is every shade of brown, and in limestone areas in particular a pale 'white' or 'silver' variety, occasionally with a distinct pink tinge when growing over basaltic rock. Mosaic disease, to which it is rather prone, particularly in damp situations, bleaches the bark and patterns it with black veins, giving a most striking appearance. If cut in the early stages of the attack the shanks are still workable. On occasion, too, shanks are found with pale bark pebbledashed with lichen. When removed carefully with fine steel wool or better still nail brush, soap and water, the bark is usually enhanced with fine blotches and capillaries of various shades of green, making possibly the most attractive of all the variations.

Many shanks are covered with fine bark flakes but this dandruff effect is easily removed by buffing down with steel wool. All hazels polish up beautifully.

## Holly

Holly would probably be more popular with stickmakers if good shanks were easier to come by. It tapers quickly in small bushes but there is potential shank material in many larger growths. Unfortunately of course in such situations it is not only most difficult to identify a suitable shank length but also to extract it from the bush!

Many shanks when cut have the most attractive highly polished smooth green bark but unfortunately this is transitory. After seasoning the colour fades to a dirty grey-brown shade and the bark is almost invariably badly wrinkled or even loose. Holly has a high moisture content and is a difficult timber to season. It is essential that cut ends are sealed as soon as possible after cutting (this includes any trimmed stumps of side branches) as checks or splits will appear quite quickly. After sealing some thought should be given to storage. Wood mice often overwinter in garden sheds and will nibble at holly shanks, both bark stripping and leaving teeth marks in the timber. Prevent this by hanging up the shanks by a cord. The mice do not trouble with any other kind of shank. Do not stretch the shanks between rafters as they bend.

After seasoning, the majority of holly shanks will need to be bark stripped. Parts will be loose quite often and can be peeled away but normally scraping will be required; this is much easier if the bark is softened initially. Probably the easiest way is to leave any shanks lying on the lawn for a few nights, turning if necessary every other day. A good scraper (¼in or ½in (0.5cm or 1cm) square of tool steel is ideal, or use an old pocket knife) will remove the softened bark easily enough, although you will normally have to sand down around knots.

The timber is white, usually tinged with a greyish cast and not very visually attractive at this stage. Make up a stain with a large spoonful of instant coffee dissolved in a little boiling water and apply with a clean cloth, after sanding smooth of course. The light olive shade stain will highlight any scratches that you have missed! Further coats will give a deeper shade. You will now have a nice looking stick particularly if the knots are standing proud, but you might care to experiment with a further method devised by the professional stickmaker Leonard Parkin, to add more character to the stripped shank. When the coffee stain is dry apply a wash of black Indian ink, wiped off more or less immediately with a damp cloth; this will leave the knots and grain pattern and any watermarks standing out in various shades of grey. As a variation consider sepia shades of inks, available from art shops. If you are loathe to risk staining a stripped shank upon which you have spent some time, have a length of prepared holly stick for experimentation, but bear in mind of course that the watermark configuration and the area around the knots will vary considerably.

Holly, like blackthorn, is a fine close-grained timber and rather heavy. The bark and underbark too are quite thick and as you will almost certainly be debarking eventually this must be borne in mind when diameter is considered whilst cutting. As with blackthorn, too, a good percentage of shanks will have an oval cross-section.

The finished shank takes a fine polish.

# OTHER SHANK WOODS

Several other woods are used occasionally in stickmaking; all have merit of some sort, the main criterion being usually their intermittent availability. No doubt novelty also enters into it.

## Alder

Widespread; flourishing in moist or wet conditions. Sends up long straight lengths, usually with few side shoots. Has a high moisture content but the bark does not wrinkle as badly as holly during seasoning. The bark is uninteresting but rub down with steel wool and you will find the underbark a pleasant reddish-brown shade. Very light after seasoning but strong enough to provide decent stick material.

## Conifers

These are frowned upon for stickmaking but I have made up several from Norway spruce (Christmas tree). The bark is exceptionally coarse but when stripped after seasoning leaves the shank stained a rather nice red mahogany shade. Very lightweight but also very tough. It does not polish and resists varnish. Minor eruptions of resin occasionally break through the wood surface after seasoning, also after heating, if straightening.

Occasionally a shortish shank length of yew, another conifer, can be found. The bark again is too rough to handle comfortably and needs removing. The timber at this stage unfortunately does not have the rich coloration of the older wood but is a reasonably attractive red-brown shade.

## Fruit Wood

All fruit wood (apple; cherry; plum; and so on) makes quite good shanks if it can be obtained in suitable lengths. It is prone to taper quickly and normally has numerous spurs or side shoots. Most of the bark shades are nondescript but cherry and plum can rival blackthorn for coloration at times. All take a good polish and are best with knots left standing proud. Like holly, fruit wood produces many oval shanks.

## Hawthorn

This is the commonest hedgerow timber but not often considered for shanks, probably because it rarely draws up to a decent length without too drastic a taper. The smooth grey bark also does not impress. The wood resembles blackthorn being tight-grained and heavy, quite often oval in cross-section, and with numerous side shoots. However if you can obtain a well-balanced shank, trim to leave the knots proud, then rub down (after seasoning) with steel wool to the under-bark, which is a pleasant red-brown shade. I have seen it stained to bear a remarkable resemblance to blackthorn and indeed it has often been sold as such.

## Mountain Ash or Rowan

Another shank wood not often seen. The bark is a plain grey but redeemed by polishing well; one peculiarity is that it nearly always wrinkles during seasoning, although it does not loosen like holly. However, if you lightly buff down to smooth out the wrinkles and leave the knots proud, it makes quite a presentable stick.

## Privet

This is a typical garden hedge shrub and unless allowed to grow to a good height will of course not produce shank material. Should you have access to any, cut thicker than normal as the bark is singularly un-attractive and will require removing. Often grows obligingly straight with few side shoots. The wood is whitish but turns pale cream to buff after oiling. Makes up to quite a decent stick, tough yet resilient.

# STAINING

Staining is usually required on a stripped shank, but judicious use also of the right shade can disguise, if not entirely obliterate, an unsightly extra large knot or – more commonly around the joint – where bare wood has been exposed when buffing down the handle to fit. The stain will often require more than one application to achieve a good colour match. However, bearing in mind the considerable colour range in shank barks it is surprising that the successful blending in that can be done with just two types of home-made stains. For paler shades use the coffee mix (described under 'Holly'), and for darker shades dissolve permanganate of potash crystals in boiling water. The crystals precipitate after a few weeks, especially if just small amounts of stain are made up but require only the addition of more water and perhaps a few crystals to resuscitate.

For ash and other grey barks experiment with adding white ink to the coffee mix and for an excellent blackthorn match add red ink to the permanganate mix. Use a clean rag and if doing a complete stripped shank try to avoid 'tidemarks' when overlapping. Blending of any stained area is easily done using fine steel wool.

# STRAIGHTENING

Few stickmakers will have the luxury of straight shanks after seasoning. Some will argue, not very convincingly, that shanks should be left natural, bends and all, as that is the way they have grown! It can hardly be disputed however that a nice straight, well-balanced shank is preferable to a bent, crooked one.

There's nothing difficult about straightening and quite a few bends can be corrected over the knee. Alternatively put the shank end to the ground or workbench top whilst holding it at about 45 degrees and press down with the free hand firmly against the bent portion. Better still, heat the bend with a hot-air gun or hair dryer for 2–3 minutes (slightly longer for blackthorn and holly) and then straighten as above. If heated to straighten spray heated area with cold water to set, but if not heated this is not necessary.

An alternative method, which saves the knees and is handy for using on bends near the ends of shanks where it is difficult to exert any leverage manually, is to use a straightening board. Mine is constructed from a 1ft (30cm) length of old fencing rail, 3in (7.5cm) wide and 1in (2.5cm) thick. I made up four hard rubber blocks from old car suspension bushes roughly 2in × 1in (5cm × 2.5cm) square and shaped a shallow crescent groove across the middle of each 2in (5cm) length. One block was fixed to each end of the board and one 3in (7.5cm) in from an end block. Two screws were placed through the back of the board into each block and also Araldite was used to hold them firm.

For gradual bends, lay the bent part of the stick across the further spaced blocks and place the fourth one against the bend, all gripped lengthways in a vice or Workmate. Heat the bent portion for a few minutes then wind in slowly and the fourth block will exert pressure on the bent portion until it straightens out. If the shank has a sharp bend place as before but between the nearer spaced rubbers before heating and exerting pressure. An alternative to rubber would be compressed cork – old fishing net floats are ideal.

Needless to say, don't attempt any straightening until a shank is fully seasoned otherwise it will tend to revert to

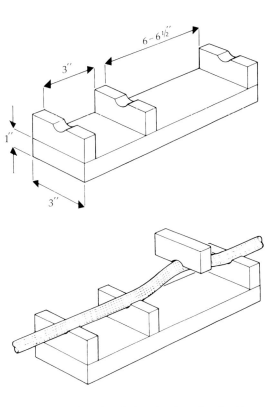

*Straightening board made from hardwood and rubber (or cork) blocks.*

its former shape. Some shanks with regularly spaced side shoots have a tendency to run out of true at each joint, resulting in several bends along the length. Each bend seems to complement (as it were) the neighbouring one and the shank feels balanced despite having half a dozen or more bends. Whilst not impossible to straighten such shanks it is perhaps better to leave well alone as there is without doubt a certain amount of character in them. They would only be good for a practical knock-around sort of stick, not show standard, naturally.

# 3   Types of Stick. All-Wood Sticks

## ONE-PIECE

### *Knob Stick*

This is the simplest of sticks, sold by the thousand each year in tourist centres in the Yorkshire Dales; Lake District; the Highlands and other favourite walking areas. Ash and hazel are the most usual with occasionally an odd blackthorn; these latter are sometimes stained black, an act which can only be described as vandalism. A blackthorn knob will, incidentally, cost twice as much as ash or hazel but could well be hawthorn, suitably dyed of course! The knob is usually fashioned from the root, trunk or stump, or a branch and will often have a deeper coloration in places than the shank wood. Whilst a larger knob may well look impressive the ease of gripping in the palm is the prime consideration so dress the handpiece down accordingly.

It is not too difficult, whatever your abilities as a carver, to fashion a crude head, Easter Island statue type, on a knob stick. Dogs, too, make good subjects; preferably droopy-eared types for damage limitation purposes. An otter, being blunt-headed, is another ideal subject, as is an owl. Realistically carved or broadly stylized, the end result can express individuality, and at the very least add character to what is a basic form of stick.

## *Thumbstick*

This is another simple type of stick. Whilst out shank cutting an occasional example can be found, but it is very rare to find the three ideal requisites: length, taper and shape together. Over, say, a 4ft (1.2m) length the taper will of course be the reverse way round, that is, towards the handle rather than away from it. The handle too will usually be badly shaped – too narrow or perhaps too splayed out; the angle of each arm may be different, or one arm much thicker than the other. The perfect thumb stick, which would have suitable length with minimal or no taper, combined with a symmetrical 'Y' or occasionally 'U' fork of a width sufficient to accommodate a thumb in comfort, is a rare find indeed. It also needs the least work to

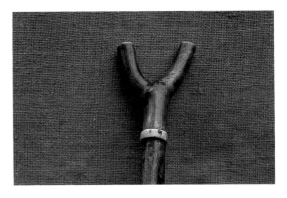

*Hazel thumbstick.*

make it ready for use; simply trim the fork arms to the preferred length, and dress down cut edges and knots. Any satisfaction in possessing a good one would lie only in the finding and not the making!

## Twisties

These are shanks that have been distorted either wholly or in part by honeysuckle which twists (always clockwise) around the growing stems and produces a spiral shape in its host, virtually by strangulation. For this reason it is much disliked by foresters, who look upon it as one of the worst of woodland weeds. They are mainly found in ash and hazel, but this is probably because they grow countrywide. It is impossible to know why twisties can be found in certain woods regularly whilst other nearby woods, apparently similar, with honeysuckle festooning most of the bushes and trees, do not produce any. Timing probably comes into it, as a young honeysuckle bine growing alongside a first-year hazel shoot would in all probability twine itself around the hazel. Depending on soil conditions the honeysuckle could easily outstrip its host in growth and not require to twist tightly for support. It is one of Nature's mysteries.

Personally I wouldn't carry a twisty myself. I would agree that they have a certain quaint charm but there is a strong possibility that the bine has bitten deeply somewhere and the weak spot in the shank is hidden by overgrown bark. They are also a nuisance in thick undergrowth such as bramble, bracken (or honeysuckle!) as they tend to snag as you are walking. However, a short length of twist in the last few inches at the top of the shank will usually make a comfortable handle as the thumb seems to fit nicely in the grooved

section. You will rarely see twisties for sale commercially – but if you do the prices will shock you.

## Root Ash Stick

This is another stick often seen for sale. It is invariably ash and is grown from seed in nurseries. When about two years old the seedlings are lifted and trimmed down to a suitable bud leaving perhaps 6in (15cm) or so of the original stem. This is laid horizontally in a shallow trench with the bud vertical. The stem after being soil covered will then develop as the rootstock and the bud grow as the shank. Side shoots are trimmed back as they appear to ensure a clean shank and good growth. Depending on soil fertility and climate the stick should be ready to lift in 3–5 years. Ash tends to taper fairly quickly when growing in open conditions and most for sale will be a yard (1m) only in length. Garden-grown ones naturally will be similar. When shank cutting in the open a suitable rootstock can occasionally be found by digging, particularly on stony soil or a rail embankment, but it's hard work doing this investigation in a thicket of ash shanks.

This is a really robust country type of stick, with no elegance about it at all, firmly resisting polishing and capable of standing up to years of hard work. Whether you find it or grow it, exercise some care when lifting the root; clear away the soil as much as possible and sever the end at about 4–6in (10cm–15cm) length. Seal the cut end, which after seasoning can be rounded off. I don't care for right-angle handles much myself but they are quite a popular stick. If you have unlimited patience you could experiment along the same lines with holly and blackthorn but I have never heard of anyone doing so.

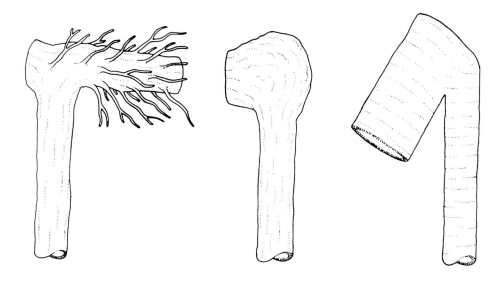

*Wood sticks: (L to R) root; knob; block.*

## Jersey Cabbage Stick

Not really wood, I suppose; but the stem *is* woody . . . This is a real curiosity which can be grown from seed and harvested the same year. Seed may be obtained from several seed merchants and spring sown. The seedlings are planted out about 6in (15cm) apart and grow rather like Brussels sprouts. Remove all side shoots to promote growth. In the Autumn, lift and trim top and bottom. Wash thoroughly and sterilize to remove any fungal growth. Hang up to dry for 3–4 months then smooth down generally. You are then faced with the problem of fitting a suitable handle, a knob type probably being as good as any. Of all types of sticks I find this one singularly unappealing, the saying 'what you see is what you get' being most appropriate. And what you get in this case is a cabbage stem . . .

It is difficult to grow in suitable dimen-

sions much longer than 3ft (1m) (and less than that in the North) and about the only redeeming features are the light weight and the strength. There are so many other good sticks to be had that the only possible attraction of this one must lie in the novelty. I certainly wouldn't wish to be seen myself carrying one.

## Bent-Handle Stick

These are a very basic umbrella handle shape and for some reason many stickmakers harbour a fancy for making one. This should present few problems as the handle shape – a half-moon – is made simply by heating the end of a long shank by either steaming in hot damp sand in a box or using a hot-air gun for a few minutes. The heated part is then bent around a former and tied in place until set. Wood crooks are made in the same way, usually a shallow notch being made near

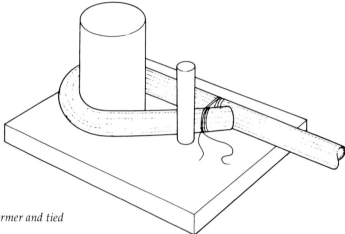

*Bent handle stick being shaped around former and tied in position.*

the end both to give the nose out shape and to allow the cord to be held in position while the heated end cools. However, the bark along the top of the crown with all of these sticks will have split during bending and there will be bunched-up bark wrinkles under the curve of the crown. Both will require smoothing down as will fibres in the wood which will also have split in the process, and the handle will be a flat oval section in shape across the crown instead of round. Neither is there any permanence about the stability in the handle shape, which will persist in retracting its curvature when wet or exposed to any heat source. Ash or sweet chestnut (debarked and stained) are the chief woods used in these types of stick. I suppose that a longish shank of stripped holly could possibly be suitable but not hazel as neither the bark nor the wood would be amenable to the heating and bending.

If I had no other stick at all I might carry one of these – reluctantly – but that is the best that I could say about them. I certainly would not waste any time or effort, or a decent shank, in attempting to make one.

## Fancy-Handle Stick

Apart from the rough carved head on a knob stick already mentioned, if you have extra wood of any shape attached to the top of a shank it is worthwhile considering a carved head of some sort. Unless you are a born carver with a finished product in mind before starting, it is as well to put the piece aside for a while. I have often had

*Plain pheasant head in holly.*

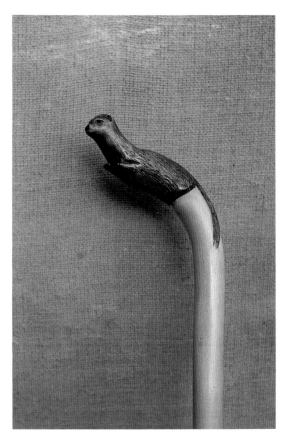

*Otter. Holly.*

won several show rosettes, been admired by many, and is the subject of numerous enquiries as to whether it was for sale. As a plain stick it had nothing to commend it, yet a bit of ingenuity and a certain skill at carving transformed it into a most attractive piece indeed. It could have just as well been carved as a stoat or weasel, incidentally.

The simplest fancy handle I ever had came virtually ready-made, needing no inspiration from me to turn out a mallard head, after fitting the eyes and trimming the bill to size. I was naturally fortunate to find it, but the duck head shape, situated at the base of the bush, could easily have been missed and cut off as a plain shank only. I always eyeball down the length of any prospective shank before cutting and find quite a few this way which can be turned into fancy handles, or the basis of rather more than just a shank length.

You don't need any great skill as a carver to do many subjects. A duck is much simpler than a pheasant for example, and a badger, stoat or weasel, also a rabbit and hare (ears a mite difficult perhaps – but could always be added) much easier than a fox. Dogs with drop ears (as opposed to prick ears) such as

odd shanks like this standing around before inspiration arrives! It may come about as a suggestion from someone else or perhaps from a book or magazine or even newspaper illustration.

A friend of mine has a stick with a handle perhaps 4in (10cm) long at right angles to the shank. This was given to him by another stickmaker who did not like the shape of the handle which came away from the shank with a sideways kink before straightening out. My friend carved an excellent reclining otter from this handle, its sinuous curves fitting perfectly into the out-of-true shape. The stick has

*Half stick in ram's horn/hazel with hare coin insert.*

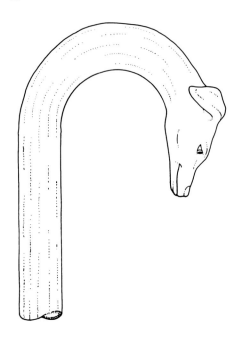

*Lurcher/greyhound dog with drop ears makes a good subject for a fancy handle.*

*Setter head in hazel.*

*Mallard head in oak.*

hounds, labradors and various terriers are not very tricky provided the ears are not too long – this is what makes spaniels difficult subjects. A collie can be a problem, but a boxer not too bad, and so on. And even a good 'natural born carver' will often refer to illustrations to ensure

*Relief carved face on shank.*

28

*Black swan in hazel.*

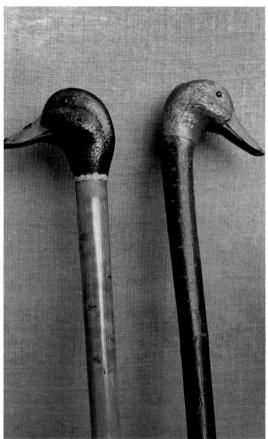

*Mallard duck and drake. Hazel.*

technical correctness. If you can borrow or already own a small model or figurine of your subject in metal, pottery, resin or whatever, so much the better. It is much easier to carve from a three-dimensional subject than from an illustration, especially if it is the same size as you require. Not so easy is to scale up or down in correct proportions.

Many carvers, some very talented, have the necessary skills to carve life-size subjects accurately but without consideration of the scale in relation to a stick handle. I have seen at shows on numerous occasions full-bodied birds carved on the necks, crowns and noses of crooks; woodpecker; tit; wren; nuthatch; thrush; and so

forth. Life-size neck and head representations of heron; cormorant; puffin and razorbill also abound – accurate representations no doubt but too cumbersome on a nominal 1in- (2.5cm) diameter shank and handle shape. One of the accomplishments of a good carver is the ability to carve to scale, enlarging or reducing, yet retaining the correct proportion. Blue tits or wrens, for instance, are small birds, with a body size of 3in (7.5cm) or so, but still look rather too bulky if carved life-size on a crook. Fancy sticks should ideally follow the architectural principle that one should

*Eagle head. Hazel.*

*Airedale and boxer dog heads. Elm.*

adorn one's constructions, not construct adornments!

However unskilled you are in carving, if the creative impulse is strong you will usually have the incentive to achieve your object eventually. The result may not satisfy a purist but can be the embodiment of highest art – to yourself. And with greater familiarity you can improve upon it. The limitations in fancy work are imposed initially not only by your own shortcomings as a carver but also by the size and shape of the piece you intend to carve. Bits and pieces such as tails, ears, eyes, beaks and ears can be added on of course as required but in the main are

more successful if the piece is to be painted. It is extremely difficult to make an invisible joint for these appurtenances in plain wood and virtually impossible to match grain or figuring.

The most effective fancy wood handles – if they are to be used (and shown off!) – are the half-head (one bend only) or crook/market stick styles. A human/dog/ animal or bird head carved from virtually a knob on the shank will of course be gripped by the carved portion in use and seems rather pointless thus as it is indistinguishable from any other knob stick. Half-head, crook and market stick are also a more comfortable carrying stick than a

*Ram's head. Hazel.*

*Owl. Elm.*

knob and have the added advantage that the carvings usually incorporate the neck or part body and reflect more truly the essential character of the subject. Ingenuity, inventiveness, imagination and inspiration can all play a part in creating a fancy stick. Two examples come to mind: one an adder carved from a natural honeysuckle-induced twist in a half stick; and another on a crook where a fortuitously placed knot hole with sawn-off small stump of a branch in its centre was situated right on the nose of the crook. The stickmaker had created from the 1in- (2.5cm) diameter stump a dapper miniature barn owl standing at the entrance to its tree hole. Both sticks reflected considerable skill at improvisation, apart from the carving expertise involved.

However lifelike the stick you are carving there is no doubt that it will not impress at all until the eyes are finished. These can be made in several ways, the simplest of which is ready-made commercial glass eyes. They can be obtained with the iris already coloured but these tend to be quite expensive. Much cheaper and giving greater flexibility in colour are clear glass ones complete with black pupil. The iris area is simply coloured on the reverse of the eye (acrylic paint dries in minutes) and this shade is 'projected' to

*Heron. Holly.*

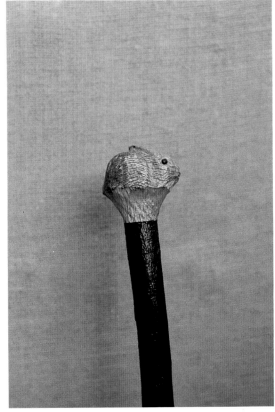

*Rabbit. Elm.*

the front. The eyes come in pairs mounted on wire. Trim the wire to ¼in (0.5cm) or so and after drilling out the eye socket, use a finer drill to drill out the centre of this socket to the same depth. When inserting the eye – after gluing the socket – feed in the wire to this centre hole and the eye will be trued up – it is not so easy manoeuvring the eye into a socket only. Glass eyes can scratch easily before the head area is complete. Put 2–3 coats of clear nail varnish over them at this stage to prevent damage. The eyes look the part but are susceptible to breakage, if handled frequently, although replacement is not too difficult. A skilled carver would carve

the eye direct on the head but a novice would hardly attempt this. It is much easier and safer to make the eyes in wood separately. Use a dowel of the same dimensions as the eye or turn one on a lathe, or make a cylinder of horn or ebony if available or softwood stained in India ink – use end grain – to the dimensions of the pupil. Insert this into the larger dowel, but colour this the iris shade beforehand. Round off the end semi-spherically.

Another method for 'home-made' eyes requires the making up of an 'eye former'. You will require a short length of metal pipe with the inside diameter the same as that of the eye. Bevel down the edge of the

*Half-head horse's head in elm burr.*

*Wood face in walnut.*

pipe until quite sharp. Make up a short dowel to fit fairly tightly inside the pipe after shaping, a concave surface on one end. Coat the depression lightly with glue and sprinkle with fine sand or carborundum dust. Coat sides of dowel also with glue then fit inside pipe so that outer edges of concave end are virtually level with the sharpened pipe rim. When the glue has set the former is held in a brace or hand drill to form the eye. An alternative to this method is to use a hollow punch, sharpening the edge if required. Naturally you will require more than one former or punch, for different projects require different eye sizes. The pupils can be inserted either as before or simply inked in but ensure that the ink does not creep into the iris.

It should go without saying of course that eyes need to be positioned carefully; many a carving has been spoiled by having 'one eye on the hearth and the other up the chimney'.

Having completed the carving it will usually be improved by staining, if painting is not considered. Hazel and holly in particular are quite light-coloured timbers and lack much character until stained. In many cases inks are a better

proposition than painting and there is an excellent colour range available nowadays. If to be painted I would use acrylics rather than oil or water-based. Varnishing afterwards is essential as paints are purely surface-based and wear badly if handled

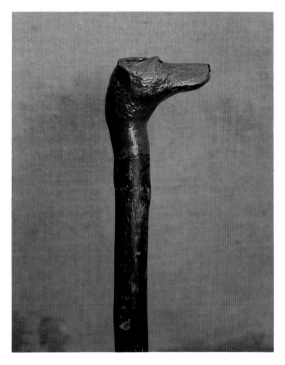

*Lurcher dog. Hazel.*

*Wood crook in holly.*

*Hazel crook.*

regularly. A satin finish is preferable to gloss and several coats much better than one. Rub down between coats lightly with emery cloth or steel wool. If the carving is finished in inks or stain use linseed oil rather than varnish; again apply several coats, rubbing in briskly each time until a fine patina appears (this won't happen overnight!). When this stabilizes, rather than slowly disappearing after each application of oil, you have a finish that will retain its pristine looks indefinitely and require only a brief rub down occasionally. Linseed is indubitably the best finish for any stick that is to be handled; the friction in the grip will actually burnish the oiled wood rather than tarnish as would happen eventually to a varnished grip.

## Block Stick

This is a stick where the handle has been fashioned from a block with suitable shank attached. The block is usually part of the trunk or branch (very occasionally root) and the larger in diameter the better as this gives greater scope in deciding the handle shape. Six inches (15cm) length is generally adequate with 1½in–2in (4cm–5cm) of this above the join with the shank. After

cutting, I seal each end with two or three coats of grafting wax and also trim off strips of bark along the length to shorten the seasoning period. A block will naturally take much longer to season than a shank, a period of two to three years being average, with eighteen months or so for thinner blocks. If the angle of the shank in relation to the block is too great, place the block end in a vice and wind in slowly to the required angle (45 degrees is about right). Then tie in position using soft cord or a strap. When seasoned, this angle will be set permanently. Conversely when you have a block which ideally should

*Block sticks in holly and hazel and ash knob. Strips of bark have been removed to reduce seasoning time.*

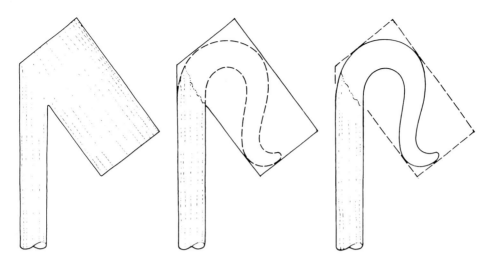

*Three stages in making crook from a blockstick: (L to R) block; planked & crook shape drawn; completed crook.*

run parallel to the shank but instead is converging upon it, pull apart to the desired position and wedge with a rubber or compressed cork block before seasoning. Either of these problem block sticks could be improved in shape after seasoning but it is obviously easier to do this initially after cutting when no heating is necessary.

Once the block is seasoned you can start

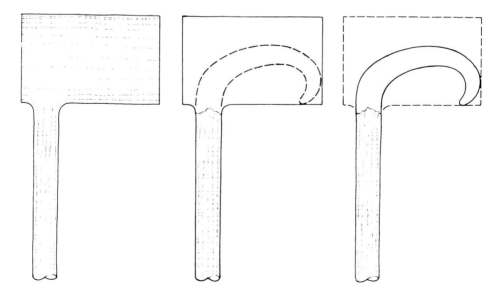

*Market stick made similarly from right-angle block.*

shaping up. But don't assume that it is ready to work just because it has been seasoning for two or three years. Many a good block has been ruined by cracks or checks appearing after work has started on it, particularly on the original cut ends. The block should not be brought into a warm or hot atmosphere at this stage; better to work on it in a cool shed or similar. If cracks do appear re-seal and season for longer. A common snag at this stage is for the shank to be out of line with the block – this could have been due to the seasoning process and not necessarily because it was that way originally. The easiest way to rectify would be to 'plank' the block in line with the shank but this often means that you will lose a good part of the block as a result, and limit your options with regard to handle shape considerably. The best solution is to heat the 2–3in (5–7.5cm) of the shank where it grows from the block, place the block in the vice and pull the shank into line slowly and hold in position with a wedge or two (have a 'dry run' beforehand to find the best position). Squirt with cold water to set. Then plank the sides. If you have a fairly heavy-duty bandsaw this will be no problem but care is needed not to mark the shank. I slip a short length of hose over the shank and wedge it firmly into the angle with the block. Alternatively use a hand saw or rasp away the sides of the block using a Surform wood rasp or engineer's files (see Chapter 1 'Tools and Tackle'). If you possess a drawknife this will work admirably but try to avoid snagging on knots which can cause it to 'jump' and gouge. Use this tool along the block *away* from the shank. A good thickness for the plank would be $1\frac{3}{8}$–$1\frac{1}{2}$in (4cm approx.) which would give a decent basis for rounding along the length of the handle.

Ideally a block stick, if it is to be used at all, should have the handle rather thicker in diameter than the 1in (2.5cm) or so of the average shank. This for strength of course. For the same reason avoid a 'rat-tailed' (that is, thinly tapered) nose which wouldn't last long in use. Once the block is planked, smooth down the surface on one side to facilitate the marking out of the handle shape.

The block dimensions and its angle in relation to the shank determine the handle shape. Don't be tempted to fashion the crown and nose of the handle tapering from the heel. This style may look very shapely in a horn handle but would be courting disaster in wood. You may find that a few templates made from perspex or clear rigid plastic sheet of handle shapes may come in handy. They will also indicate the grain and figure of the wood. Always start any pattern, whether freehand or using template, from the inside edge of the block as it leaves the shank. This is quite often covered in coarse bark disguising the line of the wood underneath so remove by rasping/filing/sanding before drawing the outline. Also before you proceed ensure that the drawn handle shape does not come right to the edge of the block apart from possibly the bottom of the nose. Removal of bark from the unplanked parts of the block and rounding up the handle shape means that some of the overall diameter of the block will be reduced. Three or four saw cuts at angles along the crown and top part of the nose will remove most of the surplus wood but again ensure that all cuts are slightly beyond the drawn handle outline, allowing for rounding up. Any small sharp segments remaining can be cleaned either by coping saw or small tenon saw cuts or by rasps.

The inside curve provides other problems of course but there are various ways to tackle these. The simplest way is by bandsaw, after drilling holes on the inside of each corner, to facilitate turning the saw blade to cut at different angles. A carpenter's bow saw is also ideal, whilst gripping the block firmly in a vice but upstanding clear of the jaws. Even a coping saw might suffice if used slowly to avoid overheating. Another method is by 'chain-drilling', which is simply following the inside curves of the handle and drilling side-by-side or semi-overlapping holes. The drilled-out section of the block is easily pushed or chiselled out when finished and the row of part curves remaining rounded out by cutting away the surplus with a coping saw or sharp chisel. If a crook, the small outcurve forming the nose is most easily shaped by drilling (clear of the outlined curve) a ½in (1cm) or ¾in (2cm) hole then completing the required outline by round or half-round rasp or even strapping.

The handle outline should now be a rough indication of the final shape but at this stage will still be flat-sided. Unless you are adept at gauging shape in rounding up, it is as well to draw a centre line along both top and bottom curves and use these as a guide when removing flats. This method obviously is not too useful if you are using strapping to round up as you will soon obliterate the lines unless very adept with the abrasive strips. When you feel that the desired shape has been reached, use progressively finer grades of emery down to (say) 240 grit to smooth down. A dab of coffee stain overall will indicate any sections needing more work. Any patches that resist final smoothing – and they are often present – should be dampened to raise the grain further then singed slightly with hot-air gun, match or candle. Sanding down afterwards will usually be successful. Knot holes, often bark overgrown, can be either left as a feature or dealt with using a small gouge or suitable size drill to form a shallow depression which can be filled with glue. This is then sprinkled with fine matching wood dust. When dry, smooth down and hopefully it should be a reasonable match. Alternatively scoop out the whole knot down to clear wood (if this is possible, depending on depth), then fill hole with clear casting resin which 'projects' the base to the surface and can be virtually invisible.

Grain direction is all important in a block – not to be confused with figuring. If there is short grain across the crown, that is, parallel to the shank, the handle will have little inherent strength. I have even seen this type break in the crown when the stick end was rapped on the floor to push home a ferrule! The crown could of course be strengthened by inserting a bolt or pin along its length but stopping short at the nose, and a disguise attempted by inserting a matching plug or false knot in the drill hole. But a nicely shaped and finished crook or market stick in ash, blackthorn, hazel or holly, with the grain running along the handle length is one to cherish. Hazel and holly will both benefit from a light stain, being rather pale timbers, but linseed oil is sufficient for the other two. You will be fortunate incidentally if you ever acquire a blackthorn block stick as they are extremely uncommon, especially in a decent shank length. If you use a block stick regularly you will almost certainly be faced at some time with a dent in the handle. Cover with a damp rag and heat with a hot-air gun and the depressed and water-softened fibres in the dent should swell back into their normal shape and remove the dent. You may need to repeat if the dent is deep (dents in cherished furniture can be dealt with similarly).

If you cut a block stick which is at right angles to the shank this will provide only a flattish basic market stick from the basic shape. Try heating the joint and placing block in a vice as described previously and pull in to narrow the angle to approximately 45 degrees or so if possible. If successful, even at the cost of some cracks in the bark, tie in position before seasoning. Alternatively this block shape is ideal for the 'half-head' (that is, one bend only) style of fancy stick. Common subjects would be fox, badger, dog head, otter, weasel or stoat, horse, duck, pheasant, and so on. In their construction little touches matter; insertion of horn beaks for instance (if to be left natural) improves upon wooden ones; likewise try to fashion life-like eyes. Leather ears are better than carved ones from the block for horse, fox, badger, and so on, which could easily break. Some subjects may need painting but good results can often be obtained with stains and inks. These can be protected by linseed oil finish but varnish paintwork. A further variation of the right-angle block is the 'T' piece where the block (usually a branch) extends across the shank equally on either side. You can fashion a good comfortable thumbstick from one of these, but if you are a carver you could consider a small tableau with this shape of block. Fox and rabbit for instance; collie and ram; ewe and lamb, and so on. None of them is practical of course but the wood in which these blocks are most commonly found, ash and hazel, are both good for carving. A fancy but functional thumbstick can be made by cutting a notch in the block above the shank end. This is opened up with a round rasp to make a comfortable thumbpiece and both 'arms' are carved with bird or animal back to back, each complementing the other. My favourite is duck and drake mallard, but you could consider fox and hound (or terrier), ram and ewe (or collie), and so on.

# TWO-PIECE

## Wood Handles

You will see many fine examples of wood-handled sticks at shows; striking colours and figuration, beautifully polished, waxed, oiled or varnished; they will often make the one-piece stick from native timbers look very mundane indeed. A crook or market stick from a hazel or ash block for instance will not command the admiration as would similar styles with rosewood or lignum vitae handles. But the exotics are there purely to be admired, there is no inherent strength in the handles, even in lignum, the hardest and most close-grained of all timbers. However attractive the exotics the majority are straight-grained unless you are fortunate in obtaining some where roots, branches or knots have resulted in change of grain direction. Even then there would probably be short-grain sections where the nose of a crook outcurves. So unless you are intending to create sticks for show or display purposes only, I would suggest confining your ambitions to thumbstick pieces or knob handles if practical sticks are to be made from most exotics. Cost too must be borne in mind as some foreign timbers can be very expensive indeed. It is also most annoying to

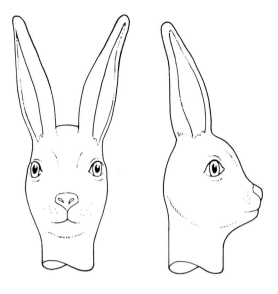

*Fancy yet functional thumbstick fashioned from block of hazel cut with two extruding branches.*

find that many are available only in boards of 1in (2.5cm) (or less) thickness which is not of much practical use in stickmaking. Burrs, where the grain structure is often distorted, are always worth consideration but as a rule are expensive also.

Native timbers in general can hardly compare in richness of colour with exotics but nonetheless some are worthy of

*Wren thumbhole handle in rosewood.*

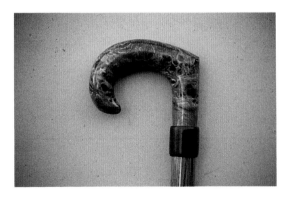

*Market stick in elm burr.*

*Wood disc market stick.*

*Running rabbit in Jarrah wood.*

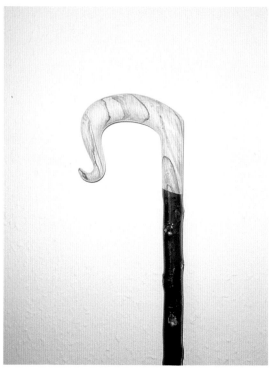

*Wood crook in elm on blackthorn.*

consideration in that respect. Walnut is the obvious example, although native-grown is not as well-coloured as French or Italian. If you are fortunate you might obtain a broken walnut gunstock where the grain and colour have been enriched by repeated oiling. Yew is a most attractive timber, only available commercially as a rule in small dimensions for turnery, with considerable variations in colour. Its chief fault is the abundance of pieces of ingrown bark and decaying areas of softwood which have healed over in growing and are invisible until work is under way. Juniper is rather similar in colour but not as a rule available commercially. It can have an exceptionally tight grain. I remember cutting a branch for use as a handle from a bush on the Lake District

fells which was just over 1in (2.5cm) thick but showed over 30 years of growth rings. Laurel can compare with walnut in colour and is a very strong timber, so too is laburnum, which often has an attractive greenish cast to it, and in really old trees will often produce a nice burr. Elm growing in limestone areas will quite likely be much redder in colour than the usual pale brown, and burr sections from these are highly prized amongst stickmakers. Quite often a water stain running through a wood will result in a rich mahogany shade and, as a variation, blackthorn occasionally runs a purple stain or tinge into the timber from the bark. Very striking indeed. Generally speaking I feel that exotics have little or no place in stickmaking – compared with native

40

*Whangee cane/hazel walking stick.*

timbers – unless for thumbsticks or purely fancy handles of no practical use. Otherwise they are over-priced, and over-rated.

The great advantage of making wood handles is just that, in fact, you can set to and make them and not be dependent on the success or otherwise of any *stick-cutting* expeditions. For instance, I cut many sticks annually, yet I rarely find any decent block sticks and am fortunate

*Elm burr crook.*

in fact if I ever come across a really good one, perhaps not more than once every four or five years. I can however cut as many blocks as I fancy with a suitable diameter short shank length attached, and after shaping up and jointing to a matching shank with perhaps a decorative antler or horn collar I have a block stick equal to any one-piece version. I doubt if there is any handle shape in a one-piece stick that could not be replicated – and in many cases improved upon – by a jointed handle. It is much easier also to work upon a handle only than one with a 4ft (1.2m) shank attached!

## Thumbstick Handle

If I see a nicely shaped 'Y' or 'U' fork, of the kind you would be looking for to make a catapult, with evenly spaced arms of the same thickness, and a neck of roughly 1in

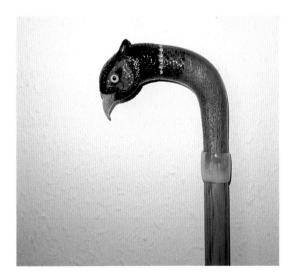

*Pheasant half head in elm burr (horn beak insert).*

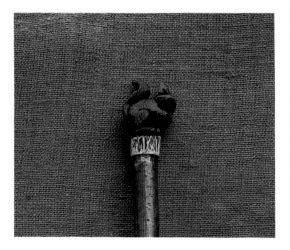

*Squirrel in ash on antler/hazel.*

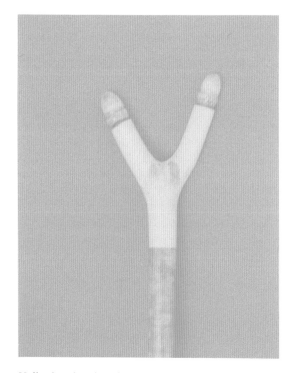

*Holly thumbstick with acorn motif.*

(2.5cm) diameter, I cut it and always have a fair selection in various woods. A nice thumbstick can be made from one of these jointed to a suitable shank, which will be well-balanced and an excellent shape; more than can be claimed for virtually any one-piece version. Insert a short horn or antler collar or spacer between handle and shank and it will look even better! And if you need to make one in a hurry and can't wait for a handle to season, having been fresh cut, simply put it in the microwave for 10–15 minutes or less on 'Defrost' setting and you will have immediate availability once it cools down. If you fear still that it may not be fully seasoned and that any remaining residual moisture may upset the efficacy of the glue, drill out the handle to accept the dowelled shank then play hot-air gun or hair dryer over the dowel for a minute or so. This method can be applied to any wood handle although a block would require longer in the microwave, naturally.

## Twisty Handle (See also section on 'Twisties' in Chapter 3)

I always suspect that a twisty shank, distorted by honeysuckle, will harbour a bark-hidden weak spot along its length somewhere. And this is usually the case. I much prefer to have a stick with twisty handle only, made by jointing a 6in- (15cm) or so shapely handle piece to a suitable shank. These make comfortable and attractive handles. I usually cut the twisty piece on the slant across a spiral at one end, the cut edge to be topped with a sliver of horn. They are naturally much easier to come across than complete twisty shanks and should be cut if possible on a plain section of shank to facilitate jointing.

An antler or horn collar can again be used at the joint if desired.

## Right-Angle Handle

If your fancy runs to a simple right angle you can often obtain suitably shaped pieces when cutting shanks. Blackthorn in particular seems to produce many of this shape. Cut off the piece with a 4–6in-(10–15cm) length to each 'arm'; it is better if the right-angle 'crown' or handle portion is of slightly thicker diameter than the neck. Round off the angle after jointing and fit with a horn cap. Shorten the crown/handle length to suit and round off the end.

# 4   Deer Antler

Antler is bone and does not have the innate attraction of horn, neither can it compare with wood in colour variation, or beauty of grain structure. But to quote from a well-known Victorian novelist, 'Plainness has its peculiar temptations quite as much as beauty . . .'. It has always been a popular stickmaking material.

Nowadays it is not particularly difficult to obtain antler. There are an estimated

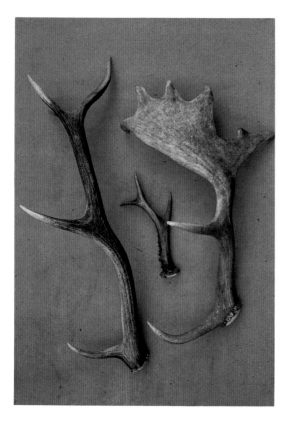

*Antler: (l–r) red deer, roe and fallow.*

300,000 or more red deer in Scotland alone, also numerous deer farms throughout Great Britain. Stags from these farms, with the natural food supplemented as necessary, and living in a stress-free environment, are much more robust animals than those in the wild, and their antler is appreciably heavier in proportion. Subsequently this 'tame' antler is much more difficult to match with suitable shanks. The antler, too, from any wild red deer in England such as those from Exmoor or the Lake District is also bulkier than Scottish wild deer. I always obtain mine from Scottish sources and consequently find that waste is kept to a minimum. Three other British deer species have antler that can be used in stick-making: roe, sika and fallow. However, they all have limitations in the variety of handle shapes that can be made from them compared with red. Roe are common throughout Great Britain, being present in most counties. Sika are the rarest with the largest concentrations being in the New Forest and parts of the Highlands. They are disliked for their habit of interbreeding freely with the red and are unlikely to be allowed to increase their numbers. Fallow are the traditional park deer and fairly common in the wild in the South up to the Midlands. Antler from park deer is usually available from the estate but little cast antler is found from wild ones in the woods. All deer eat cast antler, which is a ready-made source of calcium. Other animals too such as fox and badger do likewise and unless cast antler is found fairly quickly it will often be part chewed.

One word of advice in purchasing antler (which is normally sold by weight). Any lying outside will have absorbed moisture, which you will end up paying for. It is not unknown in fact for it to have been soaked in a water butt prior to sale! If you have any choice take antler that is stored under cover.

## PLAIN ANTLER HANDLE

### Red

Being bone, antler cannot be worked and shaped as horn can; it must be cut to shape. Red antler provides the basis of more standard shapes than any other antler.

The base of a cast antler will include the coronet, a circlet of rough warty growth. This can be oval or near round in shape and is surmounted by a dome of bone which is very rough indeed and invariably

*Pair of antler riding crop handles.*

needs smoothing. Many coronet segments too are sharp-edged and require sanding down. The first tine or point normally grows immediately below the coronet and is called the brow tine or front antler. The second tine can be closely adjacent to the brow tine or several inches away, and can be either parallel to it or at an angle. If there is a third tine it is usually separated from the second by several inches. The tip of the antler will end as a rule in either two or three points. The coronet handle is usually cut with a length of 4–6in (10–15cm) from the base, and will on occasion include the second tine depending upon its proximity to the brow tine. For some reason or other the coronet handle is always in demand and commands a higher price generally than other antler hand pieces. This popularity certainly cannot be due to any comfort in the grip because due to the coronet this is entirely absent. For a far more comfortable grip, remove the coronet growth around the perimeter of the brow of the antler by sanding, filing or using a coping saw; then smooth down the dome and the 2–3in (5–7.5cm) below right down to the underlying bone. This will as a rule polish beautifully and makes a most attractive handle with a pleasant grip.

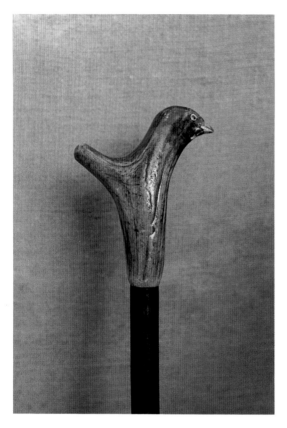

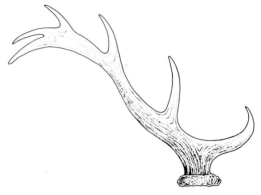

*Typical red deer six-point antler. Three or four handles can be fashioned from this.*

*Grouse head on antler thumbstick.*

Quite often the brow tine can be up to a foot (30cm) in length making it far too unwieldy for a handle. Trim off at 4–5in (10–13cm) length or to suit.

The second tine can come away from the main stem of the antler at right angles or slightly less. The normal 'walker' handle is made by cutting at an angle above the tine and allowing for a neck of 3–5in (7.5–13cm) or so. The cut edge is best capped with horn, bevelled to give a comfortable heel.

The third tine is usually treated similarly but if the antler is not a particularly thick one, and with the main stem at this point being not too disproportionate in

girth to the tine, a thumbstick shape can be considered instead. The thumb piece would need to be well-shaped of course, otherwise make a 'walker' instead. Again, trim back any elongated tine to suit.

The antler tip generally will end in two points and usually provides thumbstick handles. On better developed antler there will be three points, usually with a saucer- (or cup-) shaped hollow in front of the centre point. This could have been designed especially for a thumb rest! Any rather sharp, thin or narrow ridges between thumb-piece points can be smoothed down or widened for comfort as necessary by using a round or half-round rasp or emery-wrapped dowel. Only occasionally will the two or three points of the thumb piece be of equal length. You can choose to trim the longer one(s) to match the length of the smallest or leave in the natural state. I myself prefer the levelled up version but as I make whistles and other objects from antler tips I must admit to a slight bias!

When you have a larger antler with considerable spacing between the tines

*Antler grouse thumbstick.*

*Antler thumbstick.*

you will often be left with a piece of the main stem, perhaps 4–6in (10–15cm) long, after cutting out your handle pieces. This can be turned into quite a nice handle although at first glance it does not look too promising. Portion out along the inner edge of the antler four grooves with the edge of a file or rasp. Open these up and shape with a round or half-round rasp or file and finish with a round dowel, emery-wrapped. You now have a finger-grip handle, one of the most comfortable. The cut edge along the top needs to be capped of course, and if you use a fairly thickish piece of horn for this you can also make a thumb groove rest in this. A variation is by using the coronet end of the antler with the brow tine (also second tine if nearby) removed flush with the main stem. Make the cut edge of the tine the position of one of the finger grooves. Finally cut out with a coping saw approximately 1in (2.5cm) of the coronet segments on the opposite side to the grooves and bevel out a thumb rest in the cut-out portion to give another version of the five-finger grip.

The finger-grip handle is ideal for a fisherman's wading staff. This should, of necessity, be longer than the average stick, say 54in (1.4m) or more, and more robust, with little taper preferably. It is essential that the end is weighted as when not in use it is preferable part sunk in the water than floating and fouling the line. First fit a ferrule; this should be metal and not rubber. Copper or brass pipe is ideal. Drill out the base of the stick to a depth of 2–3in (5–7.5cm) – this will vary according to drill size, normally ½–⅝in (1.25–1.6cm). Then drill through wall of ferrule on one side only using small drill bit and push a 1in (2.5cm) nail through hole far enough to meet inner wall of ferrule opposite. Pour molten lead into drilled-out shank end – the inserted nail (at right angles) anchors the lead plug firmly and prevents slippage. Alternatively use lead shot or small ball bearings if available. These can be mixed with Araldite or other epoxy glue which again will prevent slippage. The nail is not necessary if this method is followed. If you have lead sheet you could wrap a 3in (7.5cm) or so length around the base as a weight instead and hold with two or three galvanised felt nails. This is however a rather crude method and the bottom of the lead sheet would soon wear on rocky river beds.

The wading staff normally needs a lanyard. This can be of leather but this

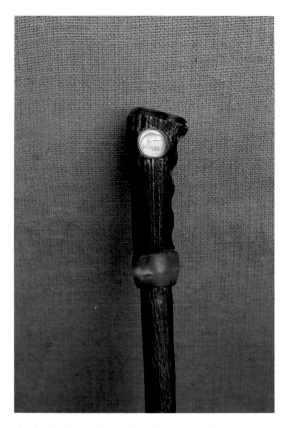

*Antler handle wading pole with salmon coin insert.*

stiffens when wet. Better is braided nylon or fine hemp cord and the length is really the choice of the individual. Fashion a loop on one end of the cord and a dog-collar lead swivel clip to the other, after drilling a suitable hole through the shank a foot or so below the handle and feeding the cord through. I have seen the cord attached to a screw-in loop or swivel attached to the shank but this is an unwieldy and not too secure method of fastening the cord.

Dog lovers who carry an antler handle stick often like a whistle incorporated in a tine. It is obviously easier to work at making the whistle before the handle is attached to the shank. The tine that is to form the whistle should be cut back

to a diameter of approximately $\frac{1}{4}$–$\frac{3}{8}$in (0.5–1cm). The core or pith will probably be showing at the cut face of the antler at this stage. Use a drill large enough to remove most or all of this core to a depth of approximately one inch (2.5cm), but bear in mind that the taper of the tine means that you will not always remove the whole of the core at the end farthest from the cut edge. Cut out with a fine tooth saw a notch $\frac{3}{4}$in (2cm) from this edge, making a vertical cut initially then a sloping (45 degrees approximately) one beyond it. The notch will need to cut through the rim of the antler just deep enough to enter the drilled-out portion. The sloping cut will have formed a crescent-shaped edge in the hollow part facing towards the mouthpiece end. There will also be a shallow air chamber in the antler just beyond the notch. Measure a length of dowel the same diameter as the drilled hole but of slightly longer length. Take a thin slice off the length of the dowel with a rise or slope in the cut from front to back. Push the end of the dowel (shallower trimmed cut end first) into the mouthpiece so that the end of the dowel, flat uppermost, is near flush with the vertical cut in the notch. The slope up of the shaved-off portion concentrates the blown air against the crescent-shaped edge in the notch facing it and this actually forms the whistle note. With luck the whistle should work the first time but if not, try minute adjustments in the dowel position both by twisting slightly or varying the depth. If still no whistle, shave off the sliced section very finely to allow passage of more air. If still no whistle note remove dowel and examine drill hole; you will probably find that a rim of core is still present. This is slightly honeycombed and will absorb blown-through air and spoil the working of the whistle. The easiest way to seal this portion is to smear either a little plastic wood or Araldite around inside the drilled hole with a spare length of dowel. (*Note.* Plastic wood sets more quickly than Araldite.) When dry reinsert the shaved dowel and the whistle should now work. Mark the position of the dowel carefully then smear with glue (except the flat part) and reinsert. Try whistle note again before glue sets. When dry, cut dowel flush to mouthpiece and round off cut edge of antler, also smooth down any rough antler along the neck of the whistle for about ½in (1.25cm) or so.

If a two-tone whistle is required drill slightly deeper into the antler initially. Just beyond the notch, drill down vertically into the extended air chamber using a ⅛in (0.3cm) or so drill. A forefinger placed over this hole whilst whistling gives a different note and individual dogs from a pair can be trained to respond.

## Roe

This is a common species but I have never come across this antler sold commercially. The main reason of course is that owing to their preference for woodland most of the antler (cast in autumn, unlike other deer, which cast in spring) is soon hidden by leaves, dying bracken and other foliage. Unless you spend a lot of time in roe-frequented woodland you will rarely find cast antler.

*Roe deer antler thumbstick. Decorative but hardly comfortable.*

Roe living north of the Midlands rarely produce antler from which a good sturdy handle can be made. At best you will find that you will have to match any from these areas with a shank of rather smaller diameter than you normally use. However, the odd buck will find his way to mineral licks and cattle cake, especially near the woodland edge. Regular access to these will result in magnificent antlers compared with other local bucks and you may come across the odd cast one now and again.

The antler is normally three-pointed and

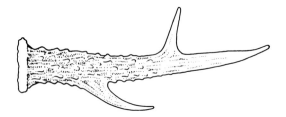

*Roe antler. Unique shape but hardly comfortable.*

can be made up into a thumbpiece only by shanking through the coronet. This requires a little care as the coronet is normally set at an angle to the main body of the antler. For at least half of its length the antler is invariably covered with a very sharp crusty growth known as pearling, and this needs to be sanded down as it makes an extremely uncomfortable grip otherwise. A roe antler handle could hardly fit the saying 'comes to hand' but it is a unique shape and consequently very popular. It is the one stick however that is normally gripped by the shank rather than the handle!

## Sika

The main strongholds of this breed are in Scotland, where there are approximately 10,000, and the New Forest. Elsewhere it is not common so you will not often get the opportunity to obtain antler. These are usually four-pointed, and roughly similar to red antlers, but with less curve along the length and

with the brow and second tine sloping at an angle from the main stem. Their tines are inclined to be on the short side but they make admirable thumbsticks as a rule. If you obtain one from a young stag it is quite an easy matter to include the brow tine and joint up through the coronet to make a thumbstick, the other arm of the thumbpiece being the trimmed-off portion of the main stem. It is rare for the coronet to be included in this handle shape and it makes quite a difference to its looks. There is little difficulty in deciding how to utilize this antler; it is usually cut as thumbpieces with occasionally a small coronet or walker style.

## Fallow

Most of this antler will originate from park deer, as little cast antler is found in the wild in the woodlands they frequent throughout the year. The antler has several drawbacks for stickmaking. At least half of the length will be palmate and useless for making practical sticks and the antler will invariably have a pronounced sideways curve along its length. There are normally only two tines and the second is often too small to be of use in anything else but a badly proportioned thumbstick, with the main stem as one arm being usually twice the diameter of the tine. The brow tine however will make a decent coronet handle although this will probably have a distinct left or right curve sideways.

If the antler is from a young buck the palmate part will not be very large and could be used to make an 'uncomfortable-but-different' type of stick. I wouldn't care to carry one myself but have seen them being used on occasion – rather self-consciously perhaps. The wider palmate section from older beasts can be scrimshawed or painted quite attractively with some wildlife illustration after smoothing down the area to be worked. Highly impractical, of course, but quite decorative and a perfect indoor stick, in fact!

*Otter scrimshaw on fallow antler. Decorative but impractical.*

## OTHER SPECIES

### Reindeer

There is a well-established herd of reindeer in the Cairngorms, maintained chiefly as a tourist attraction. Antler can be obtained from the owner/keeper. Various wildlife parks now also have deer from this herd. Both male and female deer bear antler which is normally cast at any time over a six-month period from autumn to spring. It is very smooth and bone-like in appearance and hardly any pairs are similar to others in shape. If you can have a choice, some unusual handle shapes can

*Scrimshaw on reindeer antler.*

be made from this – I have a crook shape for instance which would never occur in any other kind. The antler, from mature beasts at least, has little pith.

### Sambar

This is an Indian species, now protected, with antler superficially similar, but considerably larger and heavier, to that of red deer. The antler has little pith, being virtually solid bone and is consequently ideal for stickmaking. Obviously it is difficult to come by, but occasional specimens, usually as a mounted pair, can be had. Straight handle pieces, sold by

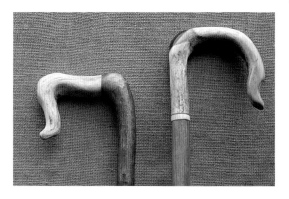

*Pair reindeer antler crooks.*

knifemakers' suppliers as handle scales, can also be obtained through trade sources but are too expensive normally for consideration in stickmaking. Old carving knives and forks and sharpening steels usually had handles of sambar antler. If they can be obtained reasonably, however battered or rusted, from junk shops or market stalls, they can often make a decent straight handle grip, with finger grooves if desired. The antler can easily be separated from the metal tang by either heating for a few minutes with a hot-air gun or immersing in boiling water. The glue will melt and the handle can be removed easily by twisting apart. Cap with horn.

Other pairs of mounted antler from various species and on occasion odd antlers can be seen now and again and are worth consideration obviously if it is felt that they could be utilized as handle material. Cost would usually be the main consideration.

# FANCY ANTLER HANDLES

Not being workable after heating, antler does not readily lend itself to fancy handles. Nonetheless there are possibilities, although naturally rather limited.

*Red deer stag head in antler.*

# FACE STICK

*Antler 'face' stick.*

The coronet circlet, however uncomfortable, has its uses – it constitutes an ideal hair line or tonsure in making a face stick. If you have a small brow tine this could represent the nose, which is a good basis for this type of stick. For the simplest version fit a pair of eyes, taxidermy ones in clear glass (suitably coloured) with black pupil are ideal. I usually use a small burr to make a few dimples in a crescent shape just below the tine 'nose'. The dimples show up white and are ideal to represent teeth. Depending upon the angle of the crescent you can have either a smiling or a scowling or downcast expression. If you want to go further, fashion a chin and shape it around each side of the jaw ending in a pair of ears. I have on occasion seen quite good representations of

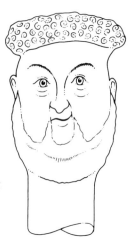

*Antler coronet utilized in making head of Henry VIII.*

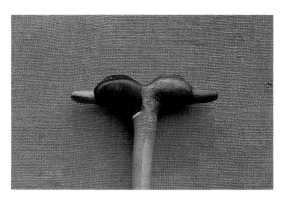

*Pair mallard wood thumbstick in ash.*

*Fox thumbhole stick in hazel/horn.*

historical figures using coronet antler – Henry VIII and General de Gaulle spring to mind – but in these cases the makers were gifted carvers and used miniature power tools with rasps and burrs in the shaping. It would be quite difficult in the hard bone material turning out such work using hand tools and any gouges and chisels would require constant sharpening as they would rapidly become blunt.

## WADER BIRD

If you have a long slightly curved brow tine at a near right angle you may have the basis of a curlew head. The tine will quite probably have a slight sideways tilt towards the tip but this can be removed and the cut-off part of the downward curve shaped instead from the thickness of the tine. The circlet of the coronet will have to be removed also but the domed bone remaining gives ample scope for fashioning the curlew head which is rather small and narrow for such a large bird. If the tine has a fair length which is straight and at the correct angle (approximately 90 degrees) to the main length of antler you could consider making a snipe, redshank or woodcock head from it. I have seen quite good ones made in this way and although they can hardly be considered practical sticks they are nonetheless considerably stronger than similar carved representations in wood.

Needless to say it is essential that as many illustrations as possible of these waders are studied before commencing the project, both for the head shapes and the plumage patterns. As a matter of interest the beak length of a curlew can vary by as much as 25 per cent, whilst many woodcock have been recorded with beaks of very short lengths down to half normal size. So even a coronet with a brow tine on the short side could still be used to carve an acceptable model.

## FANCY CORONETS

The dome of bone above the coronet can be used in scribing or scrimshawing and also painting. Ideal subjects would be small images of fox/badger/roe/rabbit/hare/otter/pheasant or duck heads, and I have also seen flowers and colourful fungi such as fly agaric in small paintings. A thistle looks good, too. All improve the

*Squirrel on antler coronet.*

pound. Suggested feathers would be jay (blue/black striped); various magpies in iridescent blue/green/purple; duck wing (speculum); cock pheasant (neck and chest); guinea fowl and game fowl; and cockerel. These can all be obtained from fishing tackle outlets, for fly tying.

Alternative inserts could be fishing flies, of which there is a vast variety – ideal for fishermen's wading staffs. Or try wren farthings or other suitable coins. Eire coins depicting hen and chickens, leaping salmon, sitting hare, deer and bull's head for instance, also a Canadian one with a moose head. Fancy buttons, too, could be utilized: I had a few in brass with a relief carved stag head motif which made up quite nicely. As the base of all the suggested cast resin inserts will be white this will not always set off the insert to its best advantage (with coins this is irrelevant). It is, however, a simple matter

appearance of the basic handle but would be prone to wear and tear unless well protected with several coats of varnish.

As an alternative to decorating as above try inserting a colourful feather in clear casting resin on the top of the coronet. Drill a shallow hole with a flat bit drill that is slightly broader than the chosen feather. Build up a low wall of tape, resin type putty, or plasticine/Blu-Tac around the hole pressing down firmly to ensure good adhesion. Dribble a small amount of the resin (after mixing in the required catalyst) into the bottom of the hole and allow to become tacky before carefully positioning the feather. Top up with more resin. When set remove the putty/plasticine then sand down the acrylic and polish with brass polish or car rubbing com-

*Carved face on antler coronet.*

to paint a more suitable colour on the base before casting the mould. With fishing flies fine silver sand can be glued to the base of the drilled hole prior to the positioning of the insert and looks particularly appropriate.

Occasionally you may obtain a pair of antler attached to the frontal plate of the skull bone. When you cut off the antler, saw carefully around the junction with the skull and you should end up with a length of solid bone immediately above the coronet. This can be of use sometimes in a carving project or perhaps for scrimshawing, especially if the coronet circlet is first removed. The only drawback to this bone is that it is usually leaning back at an angle in relation to the main length of the antler. Nonetheless it offers certain possibilities, depending obviously on length and diameter, as there will not normally be any pith present.

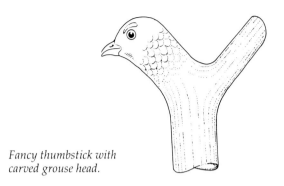

*Fancy thumbstick with carved grouse head.*

## OTHER FANCY HANDLES

All suggestions with regard to painting, scrimshaw and inserts in clear acrylic can also apply to other types of antler handle, including thumbpieces. In the case of a 'walker' handle for instance, where the antler has been cut across and exposed the pith, the base of any hole drilled will need to be sealed with glue or plastic wood prior to painting and pouring the mould. Naturally if any motif or design is to be painted or scrimshawed in an area down the side of the handle, the rough antler surface will require sanding down and smoothing beforehand to expose the white bone.

You might also care to consider relief carving, particularly if the antler bone is rather thick-skinned with a comparatively small pith or core. Smooth down again as before, then lay out the design on the exposed bone. A trout or salmon in miniature is particularly appropriate for a wading staff or a deer head on just about any type of handle. A thistle motif too would be much appreciated on a hill stick for a ghillie or stalker. Any dog owner would no doubt be proud to possess a stick with a representation of his favoured breed on the handle.

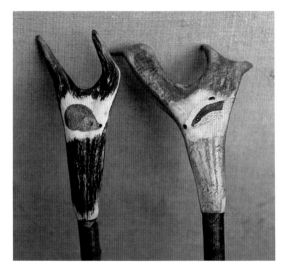

*Scrimshaw on reindeer antler.*

Practise any project beforehand on any available offcuts of antler.

# FITTING HANDLES

Antler is not always round in cross-section on the part that is to be jointed to the shank; quite often the cut end will show as a pear or an oval shape. I doubt if you would find many pear-shaped shanks to match but this is not really a problem; simply fit a shank that is near enough in diameter to the wider portion of the pear shape. Any overlap at the joint either in the antler or the shank can be sanded down to fit. If the antler is oval in section, try to match with a suitable oval-ended shank; blackthorn, holly, and fruit wood have this shape quite commonly, but it is rare in hazel or ash. Failing that, fit a shank of the same diameter as the middle section of the oval shape. The two overhung ends of antler will of course need to be tapered down to shank dimensions to give a neat appearance. A third method would be to take a suitably sized normal round shank and fashion a dowel in the normal way; then heat the top of the shank immediately below the dowel with a hot-air gun or hair dryer. When fairly hot (say, 2–3 minutes or so) place the heated part at an angle facing upwards between vice jaws and squeeze gently until the part is oval in shape. Set immediately by cold water spray. It is advisable to slip a rubber collar (a short length of car radiator hose is ideal) over the shank end before shaping as otherwise the squeezed sides will turn out flattish and spoil the effect.

Generally speaking, a handle larger in diameter than the shank – within reason, of course – can be perfectly acceptable, bevelled down at the joint to fit. A finger groove handle in fact always looks better if larger than the shank as the grooves reduce the bulky outline considerably. This is certainly not the case however where the shank diameter is greater than the handle.

If you have a hefty antler from a park deer or deer farm this will usually have a thick rim of bone with a small core. The bulk of this antler can be a little daunting but as long as the diameter is not more than (say) half an inch (1.25cm) greater than the shank, it can be matched quite successfully by fitting a counterfeit collar. You will need to cut the neck of the handle longer than usual to allow for this – one inch (2.5cm) extra is adequate. Mark off just above the (to be jointed) cut edge of the antler a 1in (2.5cm) collar line. Starting 2–3in (5–7.5cm) above this line taper down the thickness of the antler to approximately the same thickness as the shank at the top of the 'collar'. Chamfer down the top and bottom portion of the false collar to give a barrel shape. It should be noted that this method would not be successful with 'thin-skinned' antler as the outer rim of bone could not be bevelled down sufficiently without exposing the pith or core (and of course weakening the joint).

Incidentally, barrel-shaped antler collars or spacers between handle and shank on virtually any kind of stick, whether wood, horn or antler handled, are invariably effective, especially if the centre of the barrel shape is well-grooved with darker striations. This gives a pleasing contrast to the white bone above and below.

A newcomer in working antler will often agonize about removing all the core before shanking. This is not really a problem as a suitable size of flat bit drill will remove most of the core, and glue on the dowel fitting will solidify and strengthen any remnants without creating any weakness in jointing.

## FINISHING

If you have shortened any tine, whether thumbstick, coronet or 'walker' type, there will usually be darker core showing at the cut edge. This is unsightly of course but apart from that it is often not possible to round off the sharp edges of the rim of the cut without exposing more core. You can make a horn cap to glue on the cut end, which will improve the looks when polished. A slight drawback is that caps can be knocked off! A further method is to drill out the core using a suitable size drill; the drilled depth can be shallow, $^1/_8$in (0.3cm) will suffice. Shape a disc or plug of horn to fit the hole and glue in place. Sanding down and polishing – including the rim – will result in an attractive and secure finish.

All antler tips, unless already white, benefit by fine sanding down the final 2in (5cm) or so, then polishing. Try to merge the polished portion artistically into the rest of the tine and avoid a 'tidemark'.

Antler can vary in colour from virtually all-white to the darkest of browns, almost black at times, in fact. This gives considerable leeway of course in the choice of a suitable shank, more especially as the commonest shank wood, hazel, is equally obliging in its range of bark shades. I usually prefer to sand down really dark antler, also darker portions of others, to give a lighter contrasting mottled effect. If the antler is very coarse in texture, and this applies particularly to the 'pearling' on roe antler, the result may be more striped or striated than mottled and can on occasion be quite striking. Antler will take stain

readily and an uninteresting paler handle can benefit occasionally by judicious use of a choice of dye. I have used over the years coffee stain, permanganate of potash, leather dyes and inks. With all of these, keep a damp cloth handy when applying; it is an easy matter to remove most if not all of the stain if immediate action is taken. The shade of the dye after applying can look entirely different from that expected, so a trial run on an offcut from the antler used is sensible, if possible. Obstinate stain marking can be removed, when dry, with emery, steel wool, or in a well-grooved piece, with a brass bristle brush. Rarely clean when acquired, antler is usually ingrained with dirt and peat, particularly around the coronet and in the grooves. Give it a good scrub with a firm scrubbing brush and hot water with a little detergent, and it should come up clean. Any stubborn deposits should yield to an old tooth or nail brush.

Buff down finally with linseed oil. This will result in a natural finish which is superior to varnish. Although the handle may feel tacky initially the oil will soon be absorbed. Further applications can be made at intervals – you will know when to stop when the antler remains tacky.

## LEFTOVERS

In working with antler you will always have offcuts and bits left over. Don't cast them out! Over the years, with these remnants, which at first glance might seem too large or small or awkwardly shaped to use, I have made various artefacts. These include knife scales and handles; buttons for coats, waistcoats and cardigans; toggles for duffle coats; golf tees; letter opener handles and blades; fishermen's 'priests'; condiment sets; whistles; key ring additions; and so on. The palmate part of fallow antler can be mounted at right angles to a base and makes an unusual pen/pencil holder especially if decorated by scrimshawing. A set of napkin rings can easily be fashioned from suitable pieces.

And the antler dust and filings from the workshop can be used in the garden. It is pure bonemeal and an excellent slow-acting fertiliser. A visit to any stockist or maker of horn and antler goods might well generate more ideas.

# 5 Horn

Rare is the stickmaker who has not experienced the yearning to fashion a horn handle. The majority will succumb, perhaps having seen and admired intricately detailed examples of leaping trout and pheasant head, or coveted ownership of a crook or market stick in this, the most desirable of all stickmaking materials. Liking the idea of course is a considerable way from the actuality, although lack of experience and expertise can be made up for in patience, practice and enterprise. There will be many tribulations along the way, as horn can be a very intractable material, but there will eventually come a time when every stage goes well and you think that you have finally arrived. This euphoria will often only last until you have started on the next horn!

The novice may be fortunate enough to be shown some of the various methods of working horn by experienced stickmakers

*Simple walker handles in buffalo and ram's horn.*

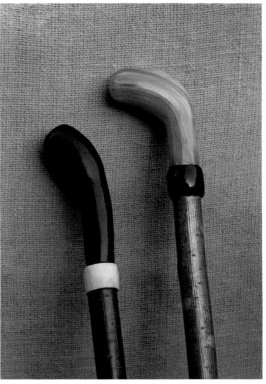

*Pistol butt handles in ram's horn and buffalo.*

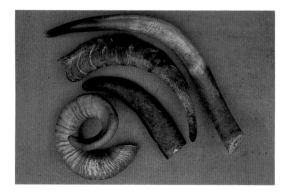

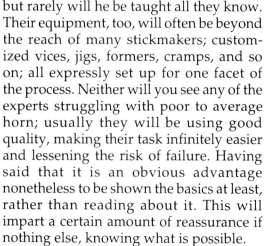

*Horn: (l–r) ram, buffalo, billy goat and highland cow.*

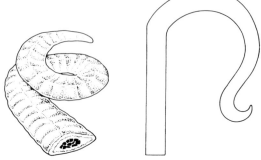

*Ram's horn and crook. The transformation is the archetypal silk purse from a sow's ear.*

but rarely will he be taught all they know. Their equipment, too, will often be beyond the reach of many stickmakers; customized vices, jigs, formers, cramps, and so on; all expressly set up for one facet of the process. Neither will you see any of the experts struggling with poor to average horn; usually they will be using good quality, making their task infinitely easier and lessening the risk of failure. Having said that it is an obvious advantage nonetheless to be shown the basics at least, rather than reading about it. This will impart a certain amount of reassurance if nothing else, knowing what is possible.

I have heard many novices say, over the years, that they have some ram's horn, and would love to make a start with it but they are frightened to do so. This is rather puzzling really as even in failure something should be learned, and ram's horn is not so rare or expensive that further (and no doubt more successful) attempts could not be ventured. However, poor-quality horn is often sold described as 'practice' horn, but I would advise against practising with this. I doubt if much can be learned from using it and it will inevitably lead to considerable frustration. Even experts could make little of it – not that

they would ever bother to waste their time in doing so. Start with as good a horn as you can obtain, travel in hope rather than expectation, and you may well surprise yourself. The transformation of the raw horn into a finished handle is like transmuting base metal into gold. Attractive, hard-wearing (near indestructible, in fact), pleasant to handle – what more can be asked for? And just about every known variety of handle shape can be made in horn – if you are clever enough.

There is considerable enjoyment in horn work; also a fair amount of exasperation and aggravation along the way. The main attribute for success in the craft is not skill but patience. Heating horn sufficiently to render it workable can be rather boring

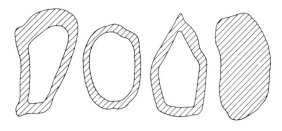

*Horns in cross-section (L to R): ram's horn; cow horn; billy goat; buffalo.*

and frustrations at the delay have ruined more prospective handles than can be blamed on inexperience. The chief satisfaction of horn work is the knowledge that you have succeeded in making the archetypal silk purse from a sow's ear! The symmetry of a crook has been described as the ultimate in functional design, natural materials and craftsmanship, which is as good a goal to strive for as any.

## RAM'S HORN

*Ram's horn crook showing diffused blood colouring.*

There are sixty-five distinct British sheep breeds in Britain, with the total number of sheep in excess of forty-two million. Not all breeds have horned rams, but nonetheless of those that do two of the hill or mountain breeds, the Scottish Blackface and the Welsh Mountain, between them account for nearly half of the overall sheep population. Thus there is no shortage of ram's horn, which has always been the most favoured for stickmaking. It is not the most beautiful of horn and in general has a limited colour range but overall it is nonetheless rather attractive. It has the considerable advantage too of being the most easily worked of any available horn. But laying hands on good quality ram's horn is not easy. This has come about for two reasons, the main one being changes in farming practices. Rams are marketed at a much earlier age nowadays

than was the case twenty-five years ago. They have bulky enough horns at this stage but if you examine a cross-section of horn you will find that the greater part is growing core covered with only a thinnish shell of solid horn. The horn will only solidify to any extent from about five years upwards whilst the core lessens.

The second reason has in general come about through financial considerations. A plain horn head stick sells nowadays for about £50 upwards, depending usually on the locality of the sales point and – naturally – the affluence of the buyer. There are a number of professional stickmakers (both full- and part-time) in the country who buy horn in bulk from abattoirs and other contacts. Naturally they want the best, not only for the end results, but also because it is much quicker and easier to work than with poorer quality. Obviously this makes it more difficult for the average few-sticks-a-year maker to obtain his essential raw material. The only advice I could offer in these circumstances is to ask around any likely sources, even when on holiday. The offer of a stick, too, will often open one or two doors, but beware any suggestion along the lines of accepting a pair of horns in exchange for making a stick with one of them. If there was a strong chance of further supplies of horn being made available as a result perhaps this could prove reasonable. But being left with one horn for your own use after spending hours making up the other horn to part with in exchange is by no means a bargain. When I lived in the Lake District in the seventies the 'exchange rate' for a stick – which was reasonable I thought at that time – was four horns; good ones, too. This then dropped to three, and just before I moved a few years ago it was down to a pair of horns. There were few tempted at that rate.

Most horn from abattoirs will obviously be fresh when obtained and it is sensible to date it, as all horn needs to season for about a year before use. Try to find out if possible approximately when any other horn obtained left the ram. Using horn before seasoning will result in distortion to your handle as it tries to revert to its original shape. Microwave heating prior to shaping up speeds up the seasoning process but I would not care to speculate as to the period involved. Remove any core from fresh horn as soon as possible. Try rapping the cut edge of the horn on the edge of the vice or a kerbstone; obstinate cases can be heated for a few minutes in boiling water or by hot-air gun to soften the horn. Then place heated portion

lengthways in a vice to loosen the core before removal.

Horn can be stored virtually anywhere; stone or paved floor; wood floor; bagged, boxed or loose, it matters little whether it is indoors or outdoors. Many dogs however find horn – and antler also – attractive for chewing, so ensure that they do not have access to it.

All horn varies in both overall length and bulk, depending initially upon the breed and then the feeding and general health of the ram. Length is important only when equated with solidity; a horn from a young ram can be of near similar dimensions to that from an older ram but with core removed will reveal a considerable hollow area. Bulk too is not so important for many styles of handle where the size can actually create difficulties in shaping up. Quite a considerable amount of surplus horn may have to be removed in some instances, and often the only advantage in the size lies in the possibility of cutting out the neck and part crown from solid horn without the tasks of heating, squeezing up and bending, and so on. Conversely of course this will lessen considerably the pleasure in working the horn, the main essence of which lies in the very heating and subsequent shaping of the original.

At the base, ram's horn will usually be roughly triangular in cross-section with rounded corners. Two of the sides will normally be convex in outline with the third concave. There will be an outcurl along the length of the horn from about halfway towards the tip. The horn will taper considerably along the length, sometimes down to a tip of less than ½in (1.25cm). The majority of horns obtained will have a hollow portion of various depths at the base. A reasonably good horn for working would have a hollow of up to 4in (10cm) or so with the rim of horn at least ¼in (0.6cm) thick (one side will normally be considerably thicker than this). There will usually be rough crusty hollows and fissures in the horn and occasionally delaminated sections usually filled with dirt. Diameter at the base would be 2in (5cm) or so.

The most difficult type of horn to work with will have both a long concave section and thin out considerably towards the tip, where it can be as much as 1in (2.5cm) wide but no more than ¼in (0.6cm) thick over the last 3–4in (7.5–10cm). Little can be done to round up the tip but if the horn has a reasonable bulk and not much hollow, rounding can be done by filing down the 'overhang' at the top and bottom of the concavity. Hopefully any remaining concave portion can be induced to round out by the judicious use of pressure applied during working. (See also Chapter 6.)

The easiest horns to work with – and consequently much in demand – are those from Welsh Mountain and Lonk breeds. The Welsh is not very bulky, usually near round in cross-section (or sometimes ovoid) along the length and for some reason quite clean-looking, being fairly smooth in appearance, unlike most other ram's horn. It is not very long and usually rather small for crook making but excellent for market sticks and ramscurl styles. Many makers of trout handles too prefer this type but a tail will often need to be inserted as the horn can be very narrow towards the tip. The Lonk is a Pennine breed, mainly from Derbyshire, South Yorkshire and Lancashire. It can provide quite a bulky horn, whose main advantage lies in the absence normally of any concave portion, being fairly round in cross-section

along its length as a rule. Anyone with a good supply of these two types of horn will assuredly have an easier time with the craft than other stickmakers!

## COW HORN

This is not readily available nowadays as the majority of horned breeds are polled. About the only ones left are Highland, and it is fortunate that their horns are long and not too bulky. There are two drawbacks to working with cow horn; firstly the strong likelihood that a good proportion of the horn will be hollow. This applies even when the horns are from an old beast. The other disadvantage with this horn is the tendency to delaminate. It appears that the layers of horn which build up over the years do not meld together as firmly as, say, ram's horn. For this reason, if on cutting into a horn there is an indication of delamination in the cross-section at the base it will prove very difficult, if not impossible, to work the horn into shape without the 'onionskin' effect ruining the process. This is assuming of course that the delaminations are present within the inner circumference of about 1in (2.5cm) on any solid portion of the horn. If the

*Mallard half-head in Highland cow horn.*

delaminations occur in the horn rim around a hollow part which will be squeezed up for the neck of a handle, for instance, then obviously it would be sensible to proceed in the normal way. But do not be too surprised or disappointed if the delaminated parts work into view on the surface during heating, bending and shaping.

Unlike ram's horn, where the horn can be trimmed and thinned down considerably before shaping up, when working with cow horn it is advisable to heat up the portion to be worked without removing any of the bulk of the horn initially. This means of course that on occasion a considerable increase in heating time is required. Never try to shorten this period by heating the inside of a hollow area as this will induce delamination. A common method used as an aid in bending horn is to cut a notch on the inside edge of the horn where the bend is intended. Doing this with cow horn is almost certain to result in delamination. A safer way is to file a shallow hollow on either side of the part to be bent. When ready to start bending after heating fit a small 'G' cramp to the sides of the horn just over these hollows. This gives two advantages. Firstly it prevents the

horn bulging out at the sides as the bending proceeds, and secondly the horn that would have formed the bulges will (at least in part) eliminate the deep cracks or creases in the horn on the inside edge of the bend. (This 'G' cramp method can also be used with advantage when working other types of horn.) Keep if possible the horn core after removal and use it as a plug when squeezing up or bending any hollow portion to reduce the possibility of the horn buckling under pressure.

With the possible exception of a well-marked Jacob's, a good cow horn is probably the most striking of the lot and well worth any extra time and care involved in the shaping process. The horn is roughly of the same consistency in hardness to ram's horn and requires similar heating times. I always soak this horn in a linseed oil bath for a month or two before working and feel that the considerable quantity of oil absorbed helps with the shaping process by inducing a mite more flexibility. Because of the problems with the hollow portion of the horn it is probably advisable for anyone with limited horn working experience to restrict their handle making to the market stick shape which requires a shorter length than a crook.

The horn is normally fairly clean in appearance with none of the crusty rough exterior common to ram's horn; it will have a slight curvature along the length but rarely any pronounced outcurve. One other good point is that it is near enough round in cross-section. I do not remember any that contained blood clots, common in ram's horn.

# BILLY GOAT HORN

Like cow horn this is not easy to come by. Probably the best source for obtaining any would be to contact the secretary of any breed society for varieties that are horned. Most country shows that exhibit livestock will have classes for goats and an approach could be made this way. There are also many well-recorded herds of wild goats around Great Britain, with total numbers exceeding 10,000, and local enquiries may prove fruitful.

*Billy goat and black buffalo horn crooks.*

As with cow horn a good proportion of any horn will be hollow and it follows that it is advisable to obtain any from older animals if possible. The horn is not round as with cow horn but a flattish oval or perhaps pear shape in cross-section, and unlike ram's horn they are thicker on the inside curve. There are two distinct horn types; one sweeps in a smooth curve with an outward twist perhaps towards the tip. With the other the horn curves back from the base then spreads out sideways about halfway along the length. Both types have an undulating ridge along the rather thin shelled outer curve, some of the bumps being quite prominent. The horns often have a tendency to taper quite quickly which creates problems in deciding on a handle shape. The last third of the horn towards the tip will also quite often be fairly flat and prove to be difficult if not impossible to round up in shape. All in all, this is not an easy horn to work satisfactorily unless you are fortunate to obtain one with good overall bulk and a considerable part solid.

The type of horn where half is twisted sideways proves virtually impossible in fact to pull permanently into line with the remainder and has an inexorable tendency to creep back at an angle. This can in fact be utilized to make it up in the ramscurl style of handle where there is a sideways curl or twist. (This shape too is useful for any type of horn that is thin or 'rat-tailed' towards the tip.)

Remove the ridge humps before

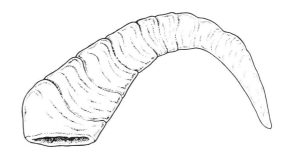

*Billy goat horn. Outer curve will have an undulating ridge. The horn will also usually taper quickly.*

working on the horn and utilize either the core or a shaped plug in the hollow portion before squeezing up. The heating time required will be approximately similar to that of ram's horn but remember that a horn from a wild billy will almost certainly be of harder consistency than that from a domesticated one. And if you have a sensitive olfactory organ I would advise avoiding goat horn as it has an extremely pungent odour when heated, rather more so than that of an ancient carpet slipper.

If you have a choice in the matter try to obtain horn from a brown, piebald or white billy as these produce nice-coloured variegated horn. Dark grey or black ones have horns that are black in the main, although these when polished have an attractive satin-like grain entirely dissimilar to the smooth rather artificial look of buffalo horn. Occasionally you may be able to obtain old trophy heads of ibex, which is the true wild goat. The horns are crescent shaped and can be up to 3ft (1m). I obtained a pair of Nubian ibex horns once but unfortunately they had come from a youngish animal and were too thin-shelled for stickmaking. But the horn when polished was probably the most beautiful I had ever handled, being a rich tortoiseshell shade. If only it had been more solid!

Incidentally, you can tell the age of goat (or ibex) by the segments along the length of the horn. A new segment is grown each year and these are separated by narrow rings which reflect the check in horn growth each winter. Horn from an older animal will be more solid and have a less hollow area than that from a young one, although the exterior size and shape can be near similar.

If you relish a challenge in horn stickmaking this is the one that will try your patience, enterprise and skill. And if you succeed the result will almost certainly not be a show winner, neither could it be claimed to be a 'once-off'. You will nonetheless meet up with very few others in the stickmaking world who own one!

There is an old Arab saying, 'If you have no other problems get yourself a goat.' This could be paraphrased for stickmakers – 'If you have no other problems get yourself some billy-goat horn'!

## BUFFALO HORN

This comes from India and is the hardest known horn. It has become fairly popular in recent years because of the shortage of good ram's horn. It is solid throughout, which means that a good portion of any stick handle can be cut out to shape

*Crook in black buffalo horn.*

without any difficult horn work being involved. The main problem lies in the bending into the rough handle shape, at the heel and the nose end of the crown. The grain in the horn is particularly dense and this results in a heating period necessary of about twice that of ram's horn. Because of the tight grain the horn does not bend easily and various methods have been devised to overcome this resistance. Because of its hardness also it has a tendency to split across the grain during bending and all in all requires careful handling at this stage.

One method, crude in its conception but quite effective nonetheless, consists of gripping the horn in a vice, heating the area to be bent and exerting leverage with a length of scaffold pole slipped over the horn. Once the required angle is reached the pole remains in position until the horn sets when cool. A further method utilizes a sash cramp gripping the base and the nose of the horn, again held in a vice and winding in the cramp until the desired angle is reached. The main problem here lies in preventing the jaw of the cramp from slipping off the rounded nose of the horn.

Yet another method involves the use of a custom-made frame of angle iron with an arrangement of two iron bobbin-like spools near the top – over which the heated horn is placed. A round bar, at right angles to the horn, is then jacked up two side posts and works as a lever to induce the bend in the horn. The maker of this device will make up one for you gladly on request – at a cost of £100!

An extremely simple and effective method of bending was devised by the late Leonard Parkin simply utilizing a wood former and sash cramp. The former is made from hardwood (oak or elm are ideal) cut with the grain, 12in × 4in × 1½in (30.5 × 10 × 3.8cm) thick. A 7in (18cm) wide × 2½in (6.3cm) deep crescent-shaped section is cut out of one side of the former (centred up). The ends of the crescent are grooved slightly to grip the horn and prevent side slippage. The heated horn is simply placed across the cut-out crescent portion and the sash cramp pulls it into the desired shape, in this instance a near right angle. The horn is left to cool and set. The second bend on the nose requires a similar former but with the crescent shape 5in (13cm) wide only to accommodate the shorter nose end of the original horn which has been bent now into an 'L' shape.

Whichever method is used it is advisable to continue heating the horn whilst bending and to wind in the pressure slowly. Any cracks in the horn which appear should be removed immediately.

Buffalo horn polishes up beautifully to a very high gloss but unfortunately this results in a slightly unnatural finish, compared by many to plastic!

*Badger half-head in black buffalo horn.*

# COLOURED OR 'GREEN' BUFFALO HORN

This comes from the Far East and, along with Highland cow horn, can be regarded as a very handsome horn indeed, the colours including green, olive and blue shades, also quite often a reddish tint reminiscent of certain types of cow horn. It is much softer than black buffalo horn, being of approximately similar consistency to ram's horn, and consequently much easier to work. The former used for the black buffalo horn can of course be utilized for this horn but I have successfully bent a shorter piece between the body of the vice (that is, *beneath* the jaws) after placing doubled over – grit out – pieces of coarse emery cloth between the horn and the vice members to prevent slippage.

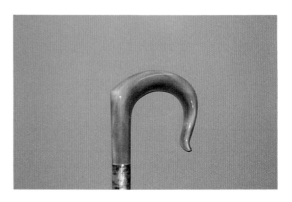

*Horn crook in coloured buffalo.*

This horn costs rather more than the black but the finished piece is infinitely more superior. That and the ease of working contribute to its popularity with many stickmakers who also find incidentally that it is favoured by many show judges.

*Crook in coloured buffalo horn.*

# 6   Making Ram's Horn Handles. Crook; Market Stick; Leg Crook; Ramscurl

A long-standing and popular way of making a horn handle is firstly to flatten the horn – after softening by boiling – in an angle iron press complete with welded base and roof plates and a loose plate used

*Ram's horn leg crook.*

in conjunction with a jack. Alternatively the horn is flattened between two large steel plates held between vice jaws. Either way you end up with a flattish horseshoe shaped piece of horn which now needs to be rounded up from base to tip.

Two advantages are claimed for this system, the first being that most of the side curl of the horn is brought into line. The other is that the concave length of one side of the horn usually present from about half-way along from the base, will have been flattened, also any hollows, humps and other irregularities in the horn. Neither claim bears close scrutiny, however, as the varying thickness of the horn from the base to the tip means that the complete length is rarely straight in line. After reheating also, in the shaping-up process, the concave face will still be evident, albeit to a lesser degree. So too will any lumps, hollows, and so on.

I used this method for several years but was never really convinced that the flattening process was absolutely essential. Look at any ram's horn along its length from the base and you will see that the outcurled portion commences only about two-thirds along its length, the major part of the horn being in line, in fact. The outcurl section can easily be brought into line by heating and sensible use of wedges. After consideration of the other

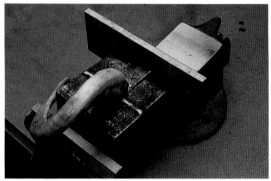

Shaping ram's horn with a 'dolly' against back plate in a vice.

Forming a neck in a ram's horn handle using channel blocks in a vice.

problem of the concave section it is often fairly evident that this can in fact be eliminated partly or wholly, by careful rasping and filing of the overhanging length of the horn at the top and bottom of the concavity. I now no longer flatten ram's horn before working.

The first essential for making horn handles is an engineer's or bench vice. Six inches (15cm) is the best size (5in (13cm) at a push) but 4in (10cm) is really too small for the job in hand. Try to obtain a *non* quick-release model as the quick-release type are prone to faults – and extremely difficult to put right. *Two vices* in fact are better than one as the two main stages in the horn work, necking up to the heel, and rounding out along the crown and the nose, require different pieces of apparatus which are easier kept apart. Having said that, you can manage quite reasonably with just the one! For shaping up the neck, and eliminating partly or wholly any hollow portion usually present, you will need to have made up (at least) three sets of channel blocks. Mine are drilled out at 1¾in (4.5cm), 1½in (3.8cm) and 1¼in (3cm). They need to be 3in (7.5cm) to 4in (10cm) deep and can be in mild steel or (better) in

alloy. For each paired block I have 'sleeves' made from ⅛in (0.3cm) thick metal pipe cut lengthways in proportion to the shape of the block pieces. These 'sleeve' inserts reduce the diameter of the horn under pressure down to the next size of block. If you can have more pairs of blocks made up at ⅛in (0.3cm) reducing sizes – instead of my ¼in (0.6cm) – then of course these pipe 'sleeves' will not be necessary.

Fit a 6in (15cm) steel plate, ½in (1.25cm) thick, to the rear jaw of the vice, held by Allen screws, which will need to be longer than the countersunk ones holding the vice jaws. Have made up in mild steel, alloy or Tufnol a cylinder (called a 'dolly') 6in (15cm) high and from 1¼in (3cm) to 1½in (3.8cm) in diameter. Make a bevelled neck, 1in (2.54cm) wide and ⅛in (0.3cm) deep in the centre, ½in (1.25cm) from one end. This

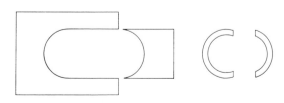

Channel blocks and reducing 'sleeve' inserts.

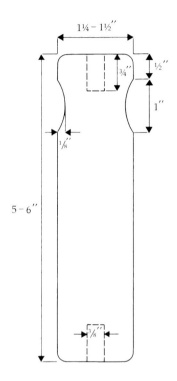

*Horn working 'dolly'.*

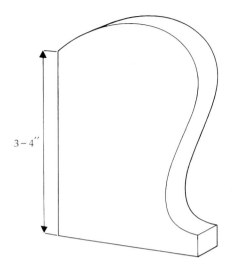

*Template for a crook.*

is your 'rolling pin' for rounding up the horn against the fixed backing plate and can be used with either the necked or the plain cylinder portion uppermost. The dolly can be held in place by various methods. Simplest is probably by drilling the centre of each end ¾in (2cm) deep and ³⁄₈in (1cm) diameter. A ½in (1.25cm) hole, ³⁄₈in (1cm) diameter, is drilled in the flat bed of the vice ¾in (2cm) in from the front jaw (if the dolly is 1½in (3.8cm) diameter). A 1¼in (3cm) length of bolt, rod or studding stands in this hole and the dolly drops over the protruding end. Alternatively, a half-moon shape piece of mild steel with 1½in (3.8cm) curvature to match the dolly can be welded on the flat vice bed in position to hold the standing dolly. A further method incorporates a 6in (15cm) length of angle iron screwed to the vice jaw, with the dolly welded vertically against the centre. A shaped bobbin drops over the end of the dolly when necessary to create a neck or plain cylinder end as required as the dolly of course is non-reversible.

You will also need a sash cramp; any size from 12in (30cm) to 18in (45cm). Have made up some hardwood formers (grain running from top to bottom). These should be 1¼in (3cm) to 1½in (3.8cm) thick preferably and should be patterned from the inside shapes of a crook, market stick and leg crook. Take a paper or card template initially from as good a source as you can. Very few good stickmakers will object to you copying their style of handle! Bevel out slightly rounded grooves along the curvature at the end of the crown/top of the nose. These hopefully will inhibit the sideways curl of the horn when heating.

Keep handy also a waterspray bottle; a large pan of cold water (unless a cold water tap is handy); several Jubilee clips from ¾in (2cm) to 1½in (3.8cm); various rasps; wedges and a length of suitable

71

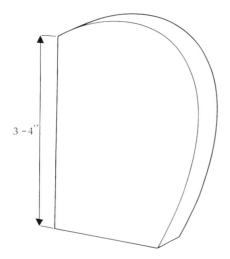
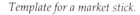

*Template for a market stick.*

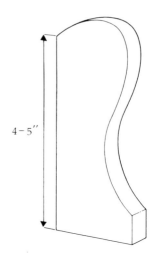

*Template for a leg crook.*

round wood rod for cutting pegs. I use a length of willow or alder branch about ¾in (2cm) to 1in (2.5cm) in diameter. This is kept outdoors generally to prevent drying out too much. Finally you will require a heat source. I use a hot-air paintstripper gun but a blow lamp is satisfactory although more prone to scorch the horn.

Before the initial heating, clean the horn up generally, removing any really rough horn, bumps or hollows (if possible); also rasp down the base of the horn to correspond to the diameter of your largest channel block (1¾in (4.5cm)) as near as possible. Have the necessary equipment laid out on the workbench – time is of the essence – to prevent undue loss of heat when working, and I even have the vice jaws unwound ready to receive the initial channel blocks. Before heating the horn, brush on the relative length some engine or linseed oil. This spreads the heat more evenly and speeds up the process slightly. Rough shape a peg from your length of willow or other rod and tap home in the hollow portion of the horn. Lea e 1in

(2.5cm) or so length protruding. This will inhibit any internal distortion of the horn when under pressure. Heat up the length of the base horn you require to make the neck, that is, 3in (7.5cm) to 4in (10cm). Depending upon the thickness of the horn cylinder rim this can take up to twenty minutes or more. Then place heated portion in the larger of the channel block pairs with the base of the horn flush with the bottom of the block channel. Fit smaller channel piece ensuring that it is level with the larger block and place in the vice so that the clamped base of the horn is visible. Wind in the vice quickly and tap the protruding end of the peg with a hammer to loosen slightly and enable more pressure to be applied. As the horn was rough shaped initially to 1¾in (4.5cm) dimensions the two parts of the block should soon come together to give a 1¾in (4.5cm) cylinder shape to the neck. Remove from the vice and tap the horn clear of the blocks. If still hot enough fit the reducing sleeves into the blocks and place horn back into the vice. Again wind up –

you will find that more pressure will need to be exerted this time to bring block pieces together. The peg may also need to be loosened again. Leave to set – squirt with cold water and after five minutes or so put horn in cold water pan. The horn neck will now be 1½in (3.8cm). Before reheating slip two or three Jubilee clips on the neck ensuring that one is pushed up tight against the top of the neck and one other around the base. These will prevent the horn from expanding however slightly on reheating. The reducing procedure is simply a repeat of the original – fit peg; heat horn; apply pressure (after removing Jubilee clips) with 1½in (3.8cm) channel blocks; and follow up with reducing sleeves, which will result in a diameter of 1¼in (3cm). You will probably find at this stage that the original flat base of the horn is now distorted and that the original hollow portion is off-centre. Centre up this hole by enlarging with a ½in (1.25cm) or ⅝in (1.6cm) drill and saw off flush the end of the horn. Replace the peg and repeat the heating and reducing process. You will often find that it is quite difficult to actually reduce the neck at this stage down to the 1in (2.5cm) or so that you require but a slightly larger neck is probably advisable in any case to facilitate cleaning up; fitting to match the chosen shank; polishing and so on. Any hole remaining in the horn base can be left as is for dowelling after drilling out or can be filled with a glue/horn dust or filings 'bodge'.

You will now need to work with the dolly in rounding up the horn along the crown and down the nose, unless of course you are fortunate to be working with a comparatively round cross-sectioned horn such as Welsh Mountain or Lonk. Start by heating the heel area, where the crown leaves the neck, and work on about 3in (7.5cm) or so of horn at one time. This area will be solid and take about the same time to heat as the thicker (but hollow) neck and base area. Test to see if workable by gripping in the vice and pulling sideways – if you can move it, it's ready! Then position the heated portion horizontally over the vice jaws – or possibly at a shallow angle – and use the dolly (normally the neck end) in conjunction with the back plate to round out the horn from the heel. The original concave section of the horn (the 'bad' side) should be uppermost as pressure will sometimes lead to the horn folding over lengthways and exacerbating any concavity, and you will obviously try to correct this as soon as it is seen. Once satisfied with the shape, cool quickly in cold water to set. Before heating the next section, fix a Jubilee clip tightly on the end of the last heated section to prevent re-expansion. Usually one more heating of 2–3in (5–7.5cm) should bring you to the nose area. The horn is tapering from the heel area as a rule and heats up more quickly and also a longer section can be worked from one heating. Remove the Jubilee clip and reposition at end of newly heated area. At this stage you will often find that the outcurl has started to reappear in the horn, particularly towards the nose area. It is an easy matter to heat and bring back into line with wedging but the horn will still tend to outcurl once again when the nose area is heated during the rounding-up process. All in all it is probably advisable to leave the horn outcurled until the complete horn has been worked, and then bring back into line before final shaping up with formers.

The horn is finally shaped around the wood formers. Quite often you will not be able to position the former inside the shaped horn as the 'mouth' of the handle

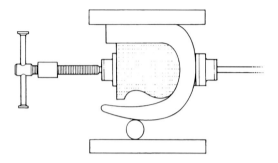

*Horn nose of crook being shaped by pressing into incurve of former using 'dolly', hammer handle or metal pipe.*

horn crown but fit one of the smaller channel block pieces across the crown initially to prevent the sash cramp putting a flat on the horn. Winding up the sash cramp pulls down the crown on to the former. Leave to set in this position. If you are using the 'nose-in' market stick former the shaping is done by reheating the nose and repositioning in the vice so that the jaws pull in the nose around the former. For the 'nose-out' crook shape heat up the last 3in–4in (7.5–10cm) of the nose and position the dolly or a hickory or ash hammer handle against the portion of the crook nose where the incurve is followed by the final outcurve. Gentle pressure will shape the horn both into the incurve and the outcurve of the nose. You now have either a market stick or crook shape, almost certainly with a slight outcurve somewhere along the length of the horn.

is too narrow. Heat the horn gently along the crown and top of the nose and it will generally relax sufficiently to enable the former to be pushed into position. Place in the vice horizontally with the jaws holding the neck and the nose lightly. Put the sash cramp over the base of the former and the

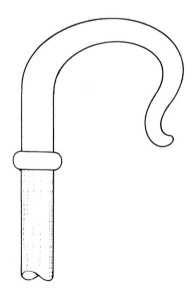

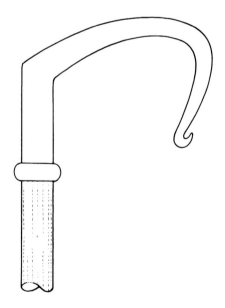

*L. classic shape crook. All curved after heel.*
*R. badly shaped crook with long thin 'rat-tailed' straight length in nose.*

*Ramscurl in black Welsh Mountain ram's horn.*

*Ramscurl in horn with setter head.*

Heat the area where the outcurve commences and pull back into line by use of a wedge or wedges. Try to ensure that any wedge does not cause a flat on any heated horn area. If the handle shape has resulted in a 'droopy nose', that is, the heel is higher than the crown where it meets the nose, heat the front of the crown and replace the former. Use of the sash cramp will push up the nose to the correct angle.

A leg crook is made in virtually the same way as the neck crook but the following points should be made:

This style has a longer neck than the market stick/crook style; this is matched by a longer nose. There is little taper along the length so a reasonably thick-nosed horn should be used. As the first bend at the heel is a much smaller radius the bending process must be undertaken slowly and carefully. The outcurve on the nose is much more gradual than the crook shape and a shaped former is necessary to apply the pressure on the horn to shape up. For a market stick you will need a horn of 10in–12in (25–30cm) length (outside edge) and for both crook shapes 14in–18in (35 x 46cm) lengths.

Yet another style of horn handle is the ramscurl. I have never seen a class for these at shows, nor will you see many carried, although a number of good stick-makers often favour one for their own personal 'carrying stick'. If you can lay hands on a suitable horn they can be surprisingly easy to make. I have made up Welsh Mountain horns in this style for instance, where virtually the only work required was in squeezing up the neck. It is also a useful shape to consider when you are faced with a narrowly tapered 'rat-tailed' horn which will never produce a shapely handle in any other style. This is the only stick I know that is either left- or right-handed, depending upon which way the natural curl on the horn runs. Most shaping (neck apart) can be done by careful heating and positioning between vice jaws or a sash cramp. If long enough, occasionally a double curl can be achieved. Ensure that there is sufficient clearance for fingers whilst gripping the handle of course. One word of advice: don't swing this stick if you are in thick cover or you will be spending some considerable time disentangling the handle from bracken, honeysuckle, bramble, and so on!

# 7 Microwave Use in Hornwork

The hornworker has always had to be innovative; offhand, for instance, I can think of six different – and by and large successful – ways of heating horn to the malleable stage. All are time-consuming and patience is an absolute essential. Modern technology can now be utilized in the craft by the use of the microwave cooker. These are expensive and the outlay could hardly be justified if one does not indulge in considerable horn work. But reconditioned ones can be obtained readily and reasonably cheaply and could soon prove indispensable after a trial period, reducing any heating times down to a quarter at least. The road to success however is fraught with problems and one can expect to encounter at times over-heated horn which is splitting, brittle and even on occasion has bubbles of molten

*Ram's horn in the microwave. The quickest way to heat horn to the workable stage.*

horn bursting through the surface! This can be a very upsetting experience for any craftsman because the situation is then irretrievable, the horn in the main having been ruined. However, there is no doubt that anyone with an enquiring turn of mind and certain amount of patience could produce a reasonably foolproof formula for successful horn bending. This of course is presupposing that he has at his disposal a sufficient and varied stock of horn for experimentation. The only problems really lie in calculating the heating times in relation to the bulk, weight, shape and of course density and tightness of the grain in the relevant horn. These problems are naturally present in conventional methods also but are identifiable then by the close visual contact required as the heating progresses.

Microwaves are produced by a magnetron which passes them into the oven. The microwaves cook by reacting on the water molecules in food; causing these molecules to agitate at an immense rate and creating friction, which equals heat. Horn of course after seasoning will contain very little, if any, moisture, and I can only surmise that as far as microwave heating goes, the reaction takes place in any oils contained in the horn. Bulk and weight naturally will require longer 'cooking' periods but bear in mind that bulk in horn does not always equate with solidity; there can be a considerable area hollow at the base. Density and grain structure are to a certain extent imponderables but horn from an older beast will have more density in the grain than that from a younger one. And a Jacob's horn, for instance, is about twice as soft (that is, more open grain) than that of most other sheep breeds, whereas most hill or mountain breeds of sheep will have denser horn than lowland breeds. The shape too of the horn is important; where it narrows towards the tip it is necessary to cover with foil about halfway through the heating process. If more than one horn is to be heated at one time arrange the thicker parts on the outside of the plate with thinner tapering parts in the centre (this would apply if several comparatively straight lengths of, say, cow horn were to be heated together). Generally speaking it is unlikely that more than one horn will be heated at the same time because work will proceed normally on an individual horn immediately afterwards. It is also important to turn over the horn halfway through the allotted time. For this reason it is easier to look upon the period decided as one of two halves and to set the timer for one half period initially. Use the 'two halves' system too in cases of tapering horn where you will need to cover the nose end with foil after the first heating period.

As far as the heat setting goes I have never, ever used any but the 'Defrost'. Any higher and I would think that you would be courting disaster. It is a simple matter after all to heat for a little longer on 'Defrost' rather than risk ruining the horn. Indeed it is probably advisable to experiment with any horn available on 'Defrost' for minimal periods, then try out in the vice for workability, replacing in the oven if required for a further period. In general the horn after heating will not be too hot to handle, unlike after using conventional surface heating methods, and indeed will sometimes convey the impression that it is hardly heated at all. A considerable bonus of microwave heating is that the 'cooking' process continues for a short time after removal from the oven. This often means that the neck of a horn can be squeezed up using two or three sets of reducing channel blocks and some of the crown along towards the nose rounded up also, all without reheating. This is a great improvement upon usual heating methods when the heat often seems to disperse rapidly before much work in shaping has been completed.

Treat with extreme caution any horn with a large 'white' present at the base. This is unformed or growing horn which has not yet achieved solidity and will almost certainly contain more moisture than solid horn and thus heat up very quickly. These types of horn present considerable problems in conventional heating methods also and microwave heating does not lessen the difficulties. A good rule of thumb for one of this type of horn is to heat only for a third or even a half less time than that calculated for a similar sized but more solid horn. If the period used proves insufficient simply heat again for a short while. Also it pays to experiment with this horn by brushing with oil (cooking or linseed) before heating. This should ensure that the outer portion of the horn will heat fairly quickly and hopefully should be ready at the same time as the white core.

A few points to remember:
1) Don't put the horn on to the oven turntable or base; use a Pyrex or ordinary china plate.
2) Ensure that the horn will not touch the sides of the oven during turntable revolutions – this will probably rule out

any long and not very curved horns such as cow, buffalo and billy goat, unless trimmed to fit.

3) *Always* heat on 'Defrost' setting (or less) and don't overtime; repeating is very quick.

Finally you will be aware that all horn has a certain pungent smell when heated, and being enclosed in a microwave oven does not lessen this, certainly not after the door is opened. Use the microwave in the garage or workshop and not in the kitchen!

A few timings (all on 'Defrost' setting) are as follows, but it must be emphasized that what has worked for me here will not necessarily work for you as horn varies considerably. Even apparently similar horns such as buffalo can have entirely dissimilar grain structure resulting from the age, health and feeding of the respective animals. These timings will give an indication only. All lengths are along outer edge.

*Blackface ram's horn*

| | |
|---|---|
| *Length* 12in (30cm) | *Base* 1¾in × 1³⁄₈in (4.5cm × 3.5cm) |
| *Hollow depth* 1½in (3.8cm) | *Average rim thickness* ¼in (0.6cm) |
| *Minimal white core* | *Tip* ½in (1.25cm) |
| | *Weight* 9oz (255g) |
| *Time* – 3 min. | |

*Welsh Mountain ram's horn*

| | |
|---|---|
| *Length* 14in (35cm) | *Base* 1³⁄₈in × 1¼in (3.5cm × 3cm) |
| *Hollow depth* 2in (5cm) | *Average rim thickness* ³⁄₈in (1cm) |
| *Minimal white core* | *Tip* ½in (1.25cm) |
| | *Weight* 8oz (227g) |
| *Time* – 2½ min. | |

*Lonk ram's horn*

| | |
|---|---|
| *Length* 11in (28cm) | *Base* 2in × 1½in (5cm × 3.8cm) |
| *Hollow* None | *Average rim thickness* ¼in (0.6cm) |
| *Minimal white core* | *Tip* ¾in (2cm) |
| | *Weight* 12oz (340g) |
| *Time* – 4 min. | |

*Highland Cow horn*

| | |
|---|---|
| *Length* 10in (25cm) | *Base* 2in (5cm) diam. (round) |
| *Hollow* None | *Small lighter core* |
| *Tip* ¾in (2cm) | *Weight* 11oz (312g) |
| *Time* – 3½ min. | |

*Black Buffalo horn*

| | |
|---|---|
| *Length* 13½in (34cm) | *Base* 4in × 1⁵⁄₈in (10cm × 4cm) |
| *Hollow* None | *Slight lighter core* |
| *Tip* ¾in (2cm) | *Weight* 1lb 8oz (0.67kg) |

*Time* – 7 min. initially, extended to 10 min.

*Note* If fortunate to obtain *coloured* buffalo horn (from the Far East) this is much softer than black buffalo horn and needs only half of the heating time.

The oven used had an automatic turntable and an output of 600 watts. If using an oven without a turntable, rotate horn by hand once or twice during heating cycle.

Be prepared for any blood clots (often not noticeable) erupting through the horn surface to form a blister. If noticed early enough the blister can be squeezed back into the horn with perhaps a suitable channel block or rubber block in the vice. I have also had a 2in (5cm) hollow in the base of a ram's horn filled with molten white core flush right up to the cut end. This had flowed back down the hollow part otherwise it would have erupted from the outer solid horn. When cooled down the base was solid. This was due to over-heating of course, so be warned – matters do not always work out so well; horn-working with a microwave can be unpredictable! If, having worked the horn and shaped up so far along but need to heat further, fit a Jubilee clip at the end of the last portion to be worked to prevent reversion to original shape during heating process.

# 8 The Half-Stick

This stick, something of a hybrid, is so called because the handle portion is part wood and part horn (or antler). It is ideal for making use of those shorter lengths of horn that tend to accumulate occasionally, the too-short-to-make-a-handle pieces that nonetheless you are reluctant to discard. Cow horn often comes into this category as a hollow horn otherwise will usually have a solid tip, but any type of horn from about 5in (13cm) in length will suffice as long as it has a base of about 1in (2.5cm) diameter at least. The wood portion is usually all in one with the shank or perhaps from a block stick which has broken across the crown.

The horn must first be shaped and as the piece used normally has not much bulk this is usually not too difficult. Bevel out a shallow hollow on each side of the incurve of the horn roughly halfway along its length. These create in effect a weak spot and after heating and applying pressure the horn should bend at that spot. The hollows are preferable to notches, particularly in cow horn, which has a tendency to delaminate. Fit a small 'G' cramp across the horn at the relevant spot to prevent the sides of the horn bulging under pressure and also pulling creases on the inside edge of the horn which may run to splits. Heat with a hot-air gun for an inch (2.5cm) or so on either side of the hollowed portion for ten minutes or so, then place horn in the vice at right angles to the jaws and wind in slowly. It is best if the horn is upcurved initially so as to monitor the part to be bent

for the appearance of any splits. When the piece has bent sufficiently to create a suitable curve, leave to set for a few minutes, then soak in cold water. If any splits appear during bending reduce pressure immediately and remove by sanding down. Reheat, then wind up again. If the horn resists bending, heat further whilst still held between vice jaws and wind in slowly. If the horn used is black buffalo it will need heating considerably longer than other horn.

Under pressure like this any horn is liable to jump out of the vice but this can be prevented by placing a pair of coarse emery sanding discs back to back with grit out – over in front of each vice jaw (that is, between jaw and horn). I glue used discs together back to back in pairs and find them extremely useful in hornwork where the curved sections often resist pressure. Remove the horn after setting and leave in cold water to cool down. Any bulges and wrinkles can be removed later.

Jointing needs a certain amount of care. Hold horn against the wood handle portion and decide if overall dimensions are satisfactory; if not, trim either or both until satisfied. The two faces to be joined must obviously be trued up but it is preferable at this stage for the base of the horn to be of greater diameter as this will facilitate the final shaping. I normally use about 3in (7.5cm) of ³⁄₈in (1cm) studding for jointing – 1½in (3.8cm) each into the wood and the horn – and obviously drilling the corresponding hole in each at the correct angle

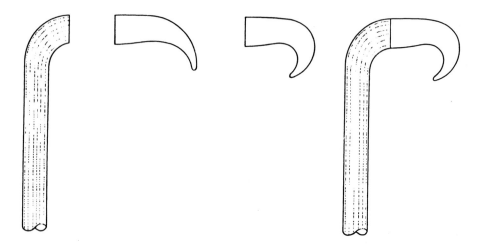

*Making the half stick: (L to R) shank including curved neck piece; suitable piece of horn; horn after bending; handle complete after jointing.*

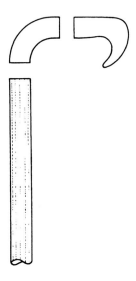

*The half and half stick comprises a shank length jointed to two suitably shaped pieces of horn or antler.*

is crucial. This is best done by two people, one at right angles to the vice whilst drilling is done, sighting to prevent any deviation from the vertical. Hold both faces together prior to gluing to ensure a true fit and trim again if necessary. Mark best position across both horn and wood with biro/pencil to facilitate correct position for jointing.

After gluing (use Araldite Rapid or similar epoxy) let the adhesive set slightly then hold together firmly after twisting both pieces to expel excess glue. Keep in position for a few minutes to ensure a really tight fit and to prevent glue line showing. Ideally this should be done either in a vice or sash cramp but in practice this is virtually impossible owing to the curvature at the heel and nose portion of the handle. Finally dress down both halves and finish in the usual way.

It is possible to make what can be called, for want of a better term, a 'half-and-half' handle. This would comprise two separate pieces of horn or one piece could be a suitably shaped piece of antler. This handle

*Pair of 'half and half' sticks – cow horn/ram's horn and buffalo/Jacob's.*

would obviously be constructed preferably from two pieces of contrasting – or complementary – horn. From the assembly and construction angle it is best to make up the handle separately prior to shanking.

Both these types of hybrid sticks are fairly uncommon but are attractive sticks in their own right and deserve more recognition. I know several show winners in fact who favour this type as their own personal stick. They wouldn't enter them in a show but they are more than happy to carry one.

# 9  Fancy Sticks

Forty years ago, when horn stickmaking was still virtually in its infancy, large solid ram's horn was the norm. Faced with such a bulk of horn which it would seem a pity to waste, some of the more artistically gifted stickmakers started producing 'fancy' sticks in addition to the plain crook and market stick. Although quite often not functional, in fact wildly impractical at times, they became popular displayed at the Shepherds' and Agricultural shows at the time. Naturally, as there was plenty of raw material available, they were all carved from the solid, that is, one piece.

Although the tradition of fancy sticks is still carried on nowadays, how does one manage with the thinner shelled ram's horn which is all that is to be had as a rule? One simply carves the fancy bits separately and sticks them on to the shaped stick handle! This practice is considered beyond the pale by older stickmakers (many of whom have stockpiled a fair amount of the older type more solid horn!) and anyone admitting to 'sticking bits on'

*Adder in ram's horn.*

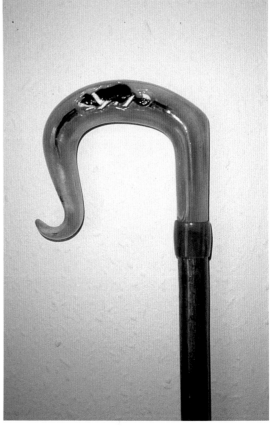

*Collie relief carving on ram's horn crook.*

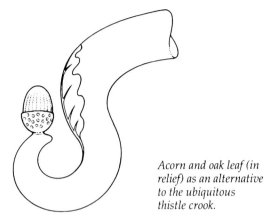

Acorn and oak leaf (in relief) as an alternative to the ubiquitous thistle crook.

Fancy horn crook – trout/mayfly.

they, as there is virtually no way to tell if any additions have been made?

A really ornately carved fancy stick is there to be admired – but not carried. They are known in the North, rather scathingly, as 'wall' or 'indoor' sticks. Yet a fancy stick can still be functional without being purely decorative. Confine your artistic carvings to the nose or front of the crown – and keep

would be subject to opprobrium from all sides. Yet the one-piece advocates practise – and even recommend – sticking bits on often enough. Eyes, ears, tails, beaks, and so on, are commonly added to their work.

The facts of the matter are of course that there cannot be any scale of such additions that are considered acceptable – it is all or nothing. Meanwhile there is a conspiracy of silence regarding the subject, but at least no show committee has been foolish enough to try to legislate in favour of the vociferous 'one-piece' lobby. How could

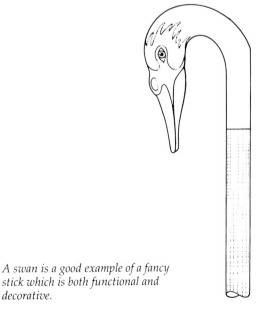

A swan is a good example of a fancy stick which is both functional and decorative.

85

them in proportion to the handle – and you can express your talent and use the sticks, without being reduced to carrying them reverently around the show circuit swathed in their protective bubble pack or other cocoons. And in your own efforts, if it is easier to stick 'bits' on – and it invariably is – then by all means do so. Have no qualms in entering them in shows either, you will be in good company – and I have yet to see any show regulation which stipulates '. . . Must be carved from one piece of horn . . .'.

## THE HALF-HEAD

This is a handle with one bend only, at the heel, and is simply a neck and a crown which is carved. It is functional yet fancy and a favourite for regular use. In shaping a crook or market stick in horn or wood it is advisable never to thin down the crown portion before shaping as in the event of any problem occurring in the nose area (blood blister; singeing; or even breakage, and so on) the crown can be utilized to fashion a half-head instead. For most subjects the crown would need to be roughly 1¼in to 1½in (3cm to 3.8cm) in diameter preferably. The overall length including the neck would be about 8in

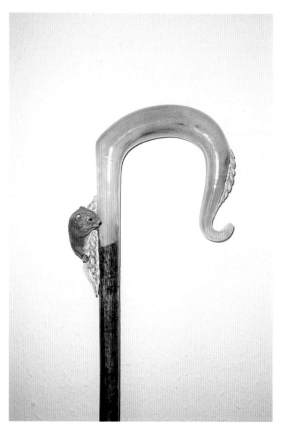

*Fancy horn crook – mouse and corn.*

(20cm), although with a shorter neck 6in (15cm) or so would suffice. Half-heads are often constructed in horn by being shanked from the nose end, giving greater bulk along the crown for carving.

Popular subjects are: otter; fox; badger; various dogs; horse; gamebirds; duck, and so on. It is also worthwhile experimenting with a trout head foremost rather than tail. In this case of course the head and shoulders only need be depicted, as a full body version would require curvature turning it into a shape that can hardly be described as within the half-head format. On one occasion I made a toucan; I can't say that I really cared for the finished

*A horse head makes a popular 'half head' subject.*

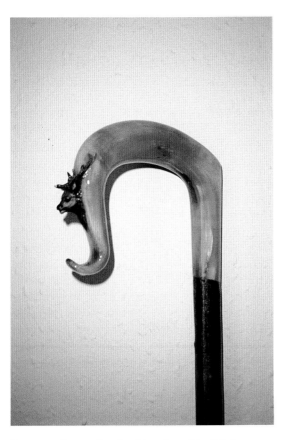

*Fancy crook – roe deer head in coloured buffalo horn.*

black buffalo horn inserts on just about anything from a pheasant to a trout, particularly when the iris is not even considered.

## Pheasant

This is probably the most popular half-head subject. This can only be due to the striking coloration as a pheasant otherwise is not a particularly attractive bird, the hen pheasant for instance will rarely be attempted. The scarlet wattles around the eye provide a striking contrast in the cock, to the shot silk, iridescent feather coloration of the head, including variations of blue, green, purple and bronze. There's the rub, of course, trying to depict such shades. However, in the past few years the problem has been reduced considerably with the introduction of pearlescent acrylic inks and paints. The ink is rather restricted in the colour range (and not too successful for hornwork in any case) but is very easy to apply, simply painting over the base colour. The paint can be either mixed with the required base colour initially or applied afterwards. I find that painting on afterwards is most successful as in mixing some of the pearlescence or iridescence is lost in the base colour. It is essential too that the base colour to be painted over with the pearlescent be as dark a shade as possible as the latter are rather light in shade and tend to stay that way unless they can take through some of the shades of the underlying colours. For example, you will need in the required areas dark base colours of purple, deep blue and green, and so on, before applying the relevant pearlescent shades, otherwise the final head colours will be much too light in shade. Suggested shades to acquire would

handle, but someone did – and offered a good price for it – so it no doubt pays to experiment!

Before commencing a half-head subject it is best to study as many illustrations of the subject as possible. A half-head is rather different from a head simply on a handle as it incorporates at least part of the neck at an angle. The head shape will often alter subtly as the neck and chin for instance become taut, often resulting in a rather narrower profile. Drooping ears too will often on some dogs not droop but pull forward to about 45 degrees to the head. Try to get the eyes correct also, particularly the colour; it is not good enough to put be Pearlescent Blue; P. Purple; P. Green, and P. Bronze.

Before painting look at some good illustrations or refer to an actual head which can be kept in the freezer indefinitely. But do not expect the freezer version to match the lustrous colours of a live bird. Note the highlights in the colours as the head moves, and avoid at all costs 'wall-to-wall' iridescence! The 'ear' feathers could be inserted into a pre-shaped head or carved from the whole after allowing for a little fullness to the back of the crown, before undercutting and separating. The beak can be a little tricky with the slightly hooked tip and the plate above the beak towards the eyes. Freezer specimens will also have the flesh around the beak receding slightly. The eyes have a distinctive deep amber or coppery coloured iris, but can be easily reproduced by the insertion of a small section of a .22 cartridge case (which is the accurate eye size, as a matter of fact) with the pupil made from black buffalo horn or ebony or other hardwood stained with Indian ink.

This is not a particularly easy subject to tackle but the great advantage of being able to use an actual (freezer) head as a model is that it is an ideal size for the half-head format. There is no need to scale up or down, which can be difficult at times even for an accomplished carver. Feathering can be completed with a small shaped bit or 'hot wire' in a pyrography tool or a small gouge.

One final tip: if the head is slightly out of line with the neck, don't bother to try to correct this; it looks more lifelike that way. But if you enter it in shows, pick your judge as some will shudder at the sight of it!

## Mallard

The drake is a regular choice for this style of handle but the duck too if well done can be a real eye-catcher. They are not too difficult a shape to carve and there is little danger of a practical stick in this style being damaged. I have seen one 25 years old in ash, still in regular use and with but vestiges of its original colour and rather battered but by the look of it good for its half-century. In fact, with a little refurbishment, it would be good enough to show.

If you see a paddling of these ducks on a lake or river, particularly if viewed from above, the main points noticeable are the differences between the individual birds both in colour variation of plumage and beak. Some drakes will have vivid metallic deep blue, almost black heads shot with purple, whilst the majority have the typical bottle green shade with lighter or deeper highlights. The beak variations show both in the colour and in overall size, usually in the width, although the graduations are slight. These differences between the birds mean that you will have a certain latitude in the handle shape and coloration.

In profile the head is nicely rounded with brow shape that corresponds roughly to the back of the head curve. The beak is approximately the same length (or very slightly less than) the head. The front view shows that the head is in two tiers with the crown only about half the cheek width. This 'stepping down' of the head width forms an eye groove, which runs in a crescent along the side of the head towards the beak. Width (full-size) at the crown is ⅝in (1.6cm) to ¾in (2cm) with the cheeks 1¼in (3cm) to 1½in (3.8cm) maximum. Duck sizes would be marginally less, overall. Top view shows that the sides of the beak are parallel with a curve in towards the end. Width of the beak should be ¾in (2cm) approximately. The eyes are roughly in line with the outer edges of the beak, with the head rather pear-shaped tapering towards the beak.

The head feathers are extremely fine and look rather like hair. Texturing can be done with a fine pointed soldering iron bit or electric burning tool, making short lines. A very fine 'V' parting tool can achieve the same effect or a small drill in a mini power tool dragged carefully to prevent gouging. It is wasted effort trying to reproduce normal head markings of small crescent-shaped feathers with this bird as they are just not visible as such! Eyes are brown and if you are a perfectionist and require the raised rim around the eyelid simply put a little extra adhesive in the drilled socket. When carefully pushed home the eyes will force out any extra glue to form the rims. The drake's beak is painted in Yellow Ochre with just a teeny addition of Burnt Sienna. The duck's beak shade varies considerably as does the plumage but is basically light shades of brown. As with a cock pheasant the drake's iridescent head colours are reproduced satisfactorily by the use of pearlescent paints. Blending is an art and possibly not easily mastered but one's efforts can always be defended by the knowledge that almost certainly there will be a similarly coloured mallard out there – somewhere!

Other ducks too can make successful half-heads; teal, widgeon, tufted and pochard in particular. Their coloration and shape all differ considerably and I have found that books on duck decoy carving, which usually include scale drawings from different angles and also invaluable tips on painting, are good sources of reference. Although all of the carving techniques refer to wood they can be freely adapted for hornwork as a rule. I have seen odd geese occasionally on sticks but find them rather ungainly in comparison with ducks, possibly because of the short and rather heavy heads.

## Badger

If you have no pretensions to being a carver you can still turn out quite a reasonable badger head without too much aggravation – or inspiration. It is more of an exercise in shaping rather than carving with none of the tricky angular contrasts in attempting a fox head, for instance. The boar has a fairly broad skull tapering in a rough wedge shape to a blunt nose. The sow has a slightly narrower head which gives more emphasis to the slight tilt upwards of the nose. The ears are not very prominent, being rough tufted crescent shapes set at the widest part of the head. Eyes are rather small and placed considerably nearer to the nose than to the ears. Nose is brown, not black as is often illustrated. Although the overall head impression is of black and white a truer representation would show a good sprinkling of grey in the fur.

You will find that it is often much easier to omit the ears when carving/shaping and to insert them later. Make shallow crescent-shaped gouges in the required places then make up the ears either with leather pieces glued into position or build up with Araldite and horn/wood shaving mix. Rough shape them before the glue sets. Texturing the fur can be done by either a small drill or burr in a mini power tool being dragged along the head or by burning in with a pyrography tool. Ears are improved by similar process as it is necessary to avoid a smooth outline.

A good shank to use for this handle

would be ash with its grey/green bark providing a nice match to the prevailing badger grey colouring.

## Fox

This is a difficult subject yet still popular. You will see many entered in shows – but few good ones. Even good carved representations are often let down by poor painting!

The head overall is quite narrow but the ears when cocked give breadth to the forehead. Some stickmakers persist in making the eyes black and this is entirely wrong. They are amber colour with a vertical pupil, similar to cats; and impart that rather sly appearance to the animal.

The ears are prominent and unless you have considerable bulk in the horn to enable carving it is best to add them. Thickish leather would do or shaped horn inserts but it is probably easier to build them up using a thick glue 'bodge' mix as with the badger. For strength it would be advisable to fix several small panel pins in place initially at each ear position on the head to give a good key for the glue. Fur texturing again is essential and this applies also to the ears. The overall colour is not red but more of a sandy rusty shade. And don't forget the white around the throat and muzzle area – many stickmakers do.

## Otter

This is quite a rare animal nowadays and even when reasonably common it was seldom seen in the wild apart from in its Scottish strongholds along the shores of the Western Isles.

With its broad, blunt head on a thick sinuous neck it makes an ideal half-head stick and a decently carved one invariably attracts considerable interest. There are few problems with the ears in this instance as they are set very close to the skull. Remember too the white or creamy/buff around the chin and throat. Although the fur is very sleek, leaving it smooth altogether would spoil the appearance; a fine texturing would be more appropriate. Overall colour has been described accurately as a rich rufous brown. I have seen one with whiskers made of horsehair – but this was on a show stick and not for general handling.

# 10    The Leaping Trout

As is apparent at stick shows, this style of handle is extremely popular, which in a way is surprising, as it is the only fancy stick handle I know which, as it is carried, is tail first! I have seen trout in the 'half-head' style of handle incorporating perhaps half of the body and head but feel that the full body and tail need to be depicted to capture the essential lithe agility of the fish. But the problem of showing a flat splayed-out tail on the round neck of a handle has never really been solved satisfactorily and until it is I suppose that the back-to-front style will remain as the favourite portrayal. To make matters worse there is a tradition in certain stickmaking circles that the nose of any stick (apart from the ramscurl style) must be strictly in line with the shank – the 'nose' in the case of the trout style being synonymous to the tail of the fish. One would normally expect that in carving, a representation as near lifelike as possible

*Horn trout.*

would be the object of the exercise. The trout handle with tail flicked sideways as it leaps is an infinitely more natural shape than the stylized rigid travesty of one with tail-in-line-with-shank that local convention demands. The latter looks crude and unlifelike ('straight from the freezer') in comparison.

A good trout handle can be made from an inferior, short ram's horn; one where it would be difficult to conjure up any other type of handle to make can often be ideal for a leaping trout. Any sideways curl need not be brought into line with the neck and filler can be used to correct any imperfections. Stickmakers who make many trout handles will in fact rarely use a first-class horn for this style as one equally as good can be fashioned from a poor one more often than not. If you are using an actual trout as a model try to obtain one weighing about 6oz (170g) or less. Any larger ones, assuming that the carving is being done to scale, will result in a handle that is too heavy and thick. I have seen salmon depicted on handles also but always felt that they too were far too large and unwieldy. A horn of 8–10in (20cm–25cm) or so in length is adequate for a good handle, whilst one a little longer can impart a really impressive sinuous shape to the body and tail. Even a shorter one can be made up into an engaging little trout as the neck of the handle need be no more than 1in (2.54cm). It is not essential to have the head projecting from the heel by more than ¼in (0.6cm) or so; although you will often see many handles with more than this, the extra projection does not particularly improve the looks. What is more important is to have the mouth positioned and shaped correctly. It is not sufficient simply to cut a 'V'-shaped notch anywhere near the front of the head and leave it like that. The mouth has a wide gape and extends quite a way from side to side; the lips too are not sharp-edged and must be rounded considerably. Eyes are well to the sides of the head and roughly level vertically with the corners of the mouth. They are large and rather protuberant and the worst way to make them is by simply inserting, as many makers do, a

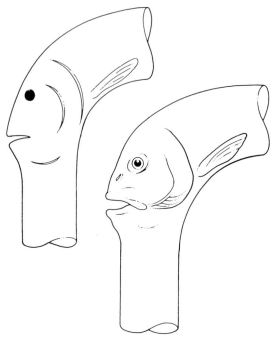

L. crude trout head with 'V' cut mouth and plain black eye. R. trout with mouth shaped and eye with pupil and iris.

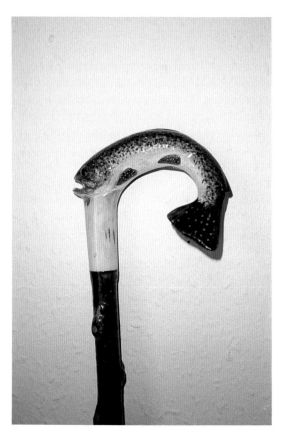

Horn trout.

round disc of black buffalo horn. Artificial ones are expensive but good ones can be made simply by drilling sockets, filling these with Araldite then inserting a pupil of buffalo horn or ebony. Both glue and pupil should be standing rather proud. When set, lightly sand down to give the bulbous 'fish-eye' look.

Shape gills and fins using a cutting wheel or fine bit on a miniature power tool, or with an engraver or pyrography tool. Alternatively use a fine 'U' or 'V'-shaped gouge. There is no need to consider carving these all to stand proud of the body, apart from the anal fin above the tail, as they would spoil the overall handle outline and incidentally ruin the grip. When it comes to the scales a very successful method is to use a small half-moon or 'U' gouge. This is naturally very laborious and one renowned exponent told me that this process always took at least six hours for completion. Recently however he has taken to using a small round head burr in a miniature power tool or engraver and lightly dimpling in the scales. The burr is held at approximately 45 degrees to the fish body. The final result is equally as good, and achieved in a fraction of the time. Whichever method is used aim for a less firm impression towards the tail to impart a subtle graduation of the scales. It is not essential to scale the complete body in the round; leave clear a band along the back and also under the belly, but again try to graduate the impression of the scales towards these points. I have seen trout made by one stick-maker who fashioned the scales, quickly and unattractively, using a gunstocker's chequering tool. This naturally made the task much simpler but the diamond mesh-grid pattern that resulted was but a travesty of representation of scales.

In the initial shaping of the fish, difficulties are often experienced with the tail, usually because the horn at the tip has little bulk. Try to get the tip really hot without scorching, a difficult process when there could well be a fair amount of white core present. Immersion in boiling water is as good a method of heating as any. Then squeeze flat in a vice, being careful to position the horn clear of any screw holes in the vice jaws. If the tail is still not sufficiently splayed out remove a little of what was the tapering horn tip and repeat the process on the slightly bulkier portion. If still not adequate, fashion a decent sized tail from an offcut of horn and joint as neatly as possible to the tip using Araldite. When satisfied as to shape, groove the tail lightly on both sides. A nice touch, to give extra life to the subject, is to give a little curvature to the tail, either laterally (across the width) or along its length; either shaping is easily done by holding the tail at the position required in the vice after warming slightly. Hold in place until set after squirting cold water on the tail.

The Rainbow Trout is constant in its colouring, this species all having virtually similar colour and markings. Brown Trout, on the other hand, vary tremendously in colour, from silver in chalk streams to some nearly black in north Northumberland rivers draining from the peat domes of the Cheviots. Others can be brown, green, blue, grey or mauve. Once out of the water however the fish starts to lose colour straightaway. Specimens from the freezer are fine for anatomical purposes but memory is the chief ally when colouring. Alternatively use illustrations from a good fishing book as a guide. There are three graduations in colouring the trout, leading upwards from the belly, through the midriff to the back. All three merge into one another and a striped effect must be avoided. It is essential to experiment – use horn offcuts if in doubt. Indian inks are probably as good a choice as any to start with and will dry immediately. The three colour layers can be merged into one another by gently smudging the joins with a wet finger, but obviously avoid 'tidemarks'. Remember too that any colour will lodge in the scale marking depressions.

A wash of iodine, watered down if necessary, is a good yellowish shade for the belly, and quite a difficult one to obtain in any other medium, although cochineal from the kitchen has its devotees. When satisfied with the overall result the markings or spots can be added. These have an outer rim of white or pale yellow, with inner spotting of black, brown or red. The simplest method is probably to use permanent marking pens, making a white or lemon spot initially and following up when dry with coloured inner leaving as little of the lighter coloured rim showing as possible. When dry, clear varnish. Using the same colouring you may with to apply further coats over the varnish after buffing down lightly with fine emery or steel wool. This of course is rather tedious but not difficult as you have the original colours as a guide, but three or four repeats will bring back the depth of colour and iridescence to the fish that was lost once it left the water.

All in all, painting your trout is an exercise in experimentation; any unsuccessful colouring is easily removed (scales apart), leaving the way clear for further trials.

# 11    Horn Thumbsticks

*Cow horn and Jacobs thumbsticks.*

You will often find that you have some shorter pieces of horn and are not quite sure how to utilize them. They will often end up as basic knob sticks or perhaps cut up for collars and spacers. Try instead this method for making thumbsticks. You will regularly see thumbsticks of wood and antler of course but rarely horn, yet a well-shaped one in a nice-coloured horn can be the best of the lot. As it is in horn, it can be made in the shape and size that you want, and for a novice also its construction will serve as an introduction to horn work.

You will need a piece 2in to 3in (5cm–7.5cm) in length with a diameter at the narrower end of at least 1in (2.5cm) suitable for shanking. It does not matter if the larger end is hollow as long as the rim thickness of the horn is at least ¼in (0.6cm). The likeliest horn you will find is cow horn – it is often also the most attractive – but buffalo horn tips are ideal, with occasionally billy goat or ram's horn, as available. The longer the piece the more scope you will have in the shaping of both neck and arms.

Portion the horn into halves by a line around the middle. Depending on the diameter of the horn at the widest end, drill a suitable size hole immediately

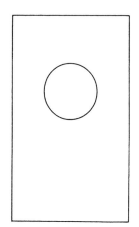
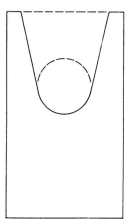
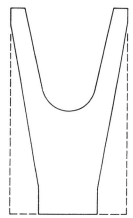

*Easily made thumbstick cut out from solid horn piece.*

above the centre line. Hole size is determined by horn width at the widest end – $\frac{3}{8}$in (1cm) hole if up to 1¼in (3cm) width and ½in (1.25cm) hole if 1½in (3.8cm) or more wide. If you have a 2in (5cm) width make a 1in (2.5cm) hole. Now cut out a slot down to this hole by two sawcuts, with the width of the slot determined by the hole size. Saw down to the outer rim of the hole using parallel cuts, not converging. Bevel down all sharp edges on the sides of the cut-out slot and around the rim of the hole, using sander, rasps, files or strapping.

Make up a selection of three or four hardwood formers (oak is ideal – cut with the grain – or Tufnol or mild steel). They should be in *depth* at least the length of the thumbpiece 'arms' – say 1½in (3.8cm) – or otherwise you may have trouble in pushing them fully home into the slot in the horn when shaping up. Again, the *width* at the top of the formers should be around 1½in (3.8cm) or so, this being ideal for an average size thumb. Bear in mind, too, that the thickness of the arms will give you a certain amount of scope in the final shaping up.

For the first shaping you will require the former with the narrowest width, otherwise splitting down the neck can occur. Naturally if you have used a wide piece of horn and have cut out, say, a 1in (2.5cm)

slot, select the former which will best suit. The aim is to splay out the arms after heating, little by little, by using a wider former each time. Fit a Jubilee clip around the neck of the horn, just below the bottom of the drilled hole, and tighten as far as possible. If the neck is oval in shape, make the clip similar by nipping lightly in a vice before fitting. Now brush oil around the base of the arms and around the top of the neck and heat this area for at least five minutes (longer if black buffalo horn). You should now be able to push the selected former into the slot of the horn at least part way by hand. Hold in position – the arms will be splayed out slightly – then replace the former with the next larger size. Push this one fully home by placing former and horn between vice jaws and wind in slowly. Pay close attention to the bottom of the drilled hole as this is where any splitting will occur. Should this happen, release pressure immediately and file or sand down to remove splits – these should not be very deep as the Jubilee clip will have prevented travel. Replace former and put horn back in vice, again winding up slowly after renewing the oil and reheating for two to three minutes. It is helpful to hold the horn near to the top and end of the vice jaws so that heat can be applied from below as well as above.

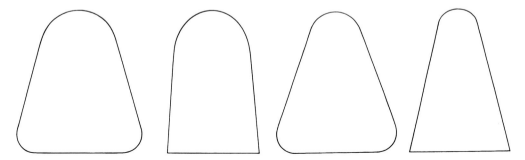

*Formers in hardwood or metal for shaping horn thumbsticks.*

Remove once the former has pushed fully home and replace it quickly with the next largest size. Again wind in slowly, applying heat as you go and looking out for splits. Finally repeat the process with the largest former, and once it has been pushed fully home, leave in position in the vice to set, spraying with cold water to speed up the process. After 2–3 minutes, remove and place in a cold water bath to complete setting. You will probably find that however careful you have been during the whole process there are still splits around the base of the hole and often on the inside edges near the base of the arms. These are virtually unavoidable once the core of any horn is subject to direct heat but the majority should disappear during final shaping. Any that remain can be filled with glue and horn dust 'bodge' trying to obtain a reasonable colour match. The core will be lighter coloured than the rest of the horn and splits can usually be camouflaged successfully enough.

If the arms are fairly thick, say at least ¼in (0.6cm) or more, shaping can be done by filing and sanding. Round off the corners at the end of the arms initially then bevel down the insides of the cut edges also. Outcurving arms are more shapely – and comfortable – than straight-up ones. If the arms are thin, try heating the top half of one, then hold it in the vice as you pull back lightly to shape an outcurve. Hold in position until set then repeat with the other arm. Should one arm be at a different angle from the other, heat the out-of-true one at the base then push in the last used former and wind up in the vice until both arms match. It may be necessary to manoeuvre the horn and former slightly at an angle to obtain the desired result. If the arms were cut from a hollow part of

the horn they may still retain a slight incurve along their length. This can be removed by heating one arm and holding the length of it in the vice to squeeze flat. Repeat with the other one. This applies only to arms that are not thick enough to have any curvature removed by sanding/filing flat, of course.

Jointing to the shank is done in the normal way but drill the base carefully for dowel or studding and stop short of the base of the thumbpiece where the original hole was made at right angles into the horn. This ensures that no unsightly top of studding or dowel can be seen at the base. Should a hole be drilled right through nonetheless, fit the studding or dowel slightly short and level the hole by a horn disc or top off with glue/horn dust bodge. If you started with a shortish length of horn, try a deepish horn collar (say 1in (2.5cm) or more) when shanking, to give the thumbpiece a little more depth. Finish by sanding down all sharp edges and round off the base between the arms to give a comfortable thumb rest. Polish horn finally in the usual way.

## SIMPLE RAM'S HORN THUMBSTICK

When using ram's horn you will quite often need to trim a piece from the hollow base prior to shaping up the neck on your prospective handle. Some of these trimmed pieces can be used to make horn thumbsticks, not very elegant perhaps but perfectly serviceable. A typical offcut would be crudely triangular in shape, with rounded corners and one side up to twice the thickness of the remaining two. This thick side will be used as the base so preferably it should be a decent thickness,

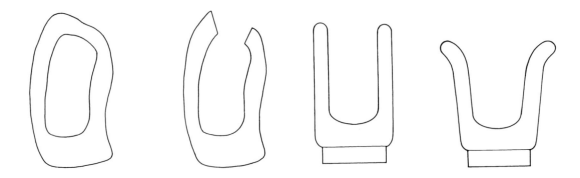

*Four stages in making simple ram's horn thumbstick.*

at least ½in (1.25cm), to allow for shanking. Saw through the apex or joint of the other two sides (that is, opposite the base side) to separate the 'arms' of the thumbpiece. Remove also any sharply incurving portions at the arm extremities. At this stage it is advisable to smooth down the piece of horn overall by sanding or filing. Ensure also that the arms are of equal thickness and length.

Heat the horn all over, ensuring that the base, being thicker, receives more heating than the arms. Feel the inside face of the horn to ensure that the heat has travelled right through. When fairly hot to the touch (between 5–10 minutes) insert a suitable size hammer handle into the horn piece or push through a tapering peg made from a short length of broom shank or something similar. Push home until the arms of the thumbpiece open out to a suitable angle. It will be necessary to grip in the vice at this stage to hold in place the wood used as pressure from the arms may ease it out of position. Wait until set (after placing in cold water) then remove the wood. Hopefully this will have rounded the base of the thumb hole and at the same time the bottom of the horn base should have flattened against the vice jaws. This will facilitate shanking. If the arms have splayed out too far and you don't care too much about the shape, replace the wood shaper back in position and reheat the arms. After 2–3 minutes place the thumbpiece arms between the vice jaws and pull in slightly around the shape of the wood before setting again. If one arm has set at a different angle from the other, decide whether it wants splaying out or pulling in. If the former, heat and pull out gently with a mole grip; if the latter put between vice jaws after heating the out-of-true arm and wind in sufficiently to pull it level with the other.

The base will probably not be any more than ½in (1.25cm) thick, sometimes less, and obviously this will hardly suffice for shanking. I find that a suitable piece of contrasting horn or a well-grooved antler disc solves the problem. It is easier to glue the extension piece to the base and make really firm by gripping in the vice until the glue sets. Then drill for dowel or studding in the usual way, but as before try not to drill right through to the base of the thumb hole. Stopping short by even a millimetre or so will save the necessity for any cosmetic work hiding the dowel or studding head. As the width of the horn at the base will have been wider than the shank, it will be necessary to bevel it down to the extension piece to give a reasonable shape. This could be done prior to jointing of course but I find it easier afterwards as the extension may need to be contoured to the shank also.

Although the looks of this type of thumbpiece will rarely match the previous one shaped by formers it does however have one advantage. It will rarely split at the base after heating and insertion of the wood plug. This is due to the two arms 'growing' naturally from the base, whereas the other has arms that are cut out before shaping. The base on this style will also be wider initially and require little shaping apart from bevelling down the front edge to make a comfortable fit for the thumb.

## FANCY THUMBHOLE HANDLE

The traditional thumbstick has two arms, usually in the 'V' or 'U' shape, but another style incorporates a thumbhole. This is fashioned from a similar offcut of ram's horn as the previous style but shanked in a reverse fashion with the thicker horn side

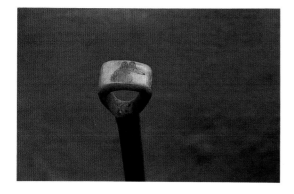

*Scrimshaw fox on ram's horn thumbhole handle.*

utilized as the top of the thumbpiece. The resulting handle can be both practicable and decorative.

Bearing in mind that even an average-sized thumb will be at least 1in (2.5cm) in diameter across the first joint, you will obviously require a decent-sized horn offcut. One of 1in to 1½in (2.5–3.8cm) width across the hollow portion will suffice, any wider would be a bonus. Put the horn piece in boiling water and soften for 10–15 minutes. Then push/drive/hammer home (being careful not to split the horn) a tapered peg with a base of at least 1in (2.5cm) round section. Insert the peg in the cut face of the horn which shows the lesser width across the hollow portion. Ensure that the peg has been pushed sufficiently home so that all of the hollow portion of the horn encloses the 1in (2.5cm) diameter section. When correctly positioned, place in cold water to set. Then carefully remove the peg, again being careful not to split the horn. Level up the thickness of both sides by sanding/filing, then dress down the top. It is not essential that this be absolutely flat, a slightly domed shape will do, although this may make any fancy work a little more difficult.

Now level the base but try not to thin down the available horn too much. Finally, clean up the horn around both sides. The base will need an extension piece as in the previous style to give sufficient depth for dowelling or studding. Glue in place before drilling for shanking using a piece of contrasting coloured horn or antler. A disc of exotic timber such as rosewood or purpleheart if available would also be suitable. A small 'G' cramp can be used to hold this in position until the glue is set or the thumbpiece plus extension could be gripped lightly between the vice or sash cramp jaws. When drilling through the base again for shanking, stop just short of the thumbpiece aperture. You may have reservations about the short dowel fitting but in practice this is quite strong enough for normal use as the thumb is pressing down upon it vertically and there is little lateral strain on the handle.

Finally, decide on a suitable subject for your fancy work on the top of the handle, bearing in mind the size and thickness of the available horn. Suitable projects could be eagle head (profile); mallard (full body or head); pheasant head; hedgehog; fox mask or sleeping fox; badger; rabbit or hare; owl; trout or salmon. Outline by fine 'V' gouge or pyrography tool or fine bit in mini power tool, then relief carve if desired. Colour as necessary. If coloured I would advise a varnish finish but this is not essential if only a pyrography scribing is involved.

Thumbsticks always have limitations with regard to shape but this type of handle offers new options to consider. On occasion, if the top of the horn was nicely bloodshot, or perhaps from a variegated Jacob's horn, it would not need any further adornment, being an attractive piece in its own right. It has the advantage of course in utilizing offcuts of horn that would not usually suggest handle material.

# 12 Colouring Ram's Horn

Ram's horn accounts for by far the greatest proportion of all horn sticks made. This no doubt reflects its reasonable availability, relatively low cost and ready malleability when heated. If there is one drawback to this paragon amongst horn it is the comparatively poor range of colour, differing only slightly between shades of straw and wheat. Blackface and odd minor breeds will show random black lines along their length; these unfortunately however are frequently only skin deep and will be buffed out when sanding smooth. Jacob's has an attractive mix of black, brown, cream and yellowish white but is often too one-sided in its colouring when shaped up. About the only other colour met with fairly frequently will be odd bloodshot sections of horn. Occasionally Black Welsh Mountain horn can be obtained but this is predominantly black with only a small segment near the base and occasionally towards the tip lighter in colour.

If you work with ram's horn a lot, it would be worthwhile considering staining or dying the horn to give a wider colour range. There are two methods devised by the late Leonard Parkin, who always had an excellent variety of horn sticks on display in his showroom. He believed in offering not only a wide choice of handles, both plain and fancy, but also a considerable colour range. There are two main colours involved, with each offering subtle minor variations in shade.

You will need two large pans; old pressure cookers are ideal. Obtain a five-litre drum of linseed oil (raw is cheaper than the refined type), also ½lb (227g) of orange shellac flakes. Fill each pan with the oil to within two inches (5cm) or so of the rim. Add two large tablespoonfuls of the

*Ram's horn market stick dyed in shellac and linseed oil.*

*Jacob's horn crook.*

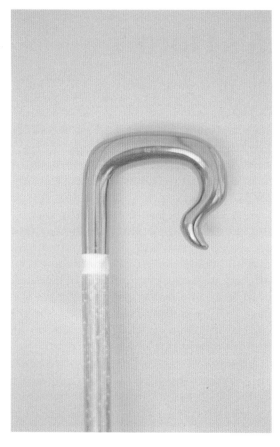

*Black Welsh Mountain ram's horn crook.*

*Blackface ram's horn market stick and crook.*

shellac slowly, stirring continuously to help dissolving, whilst bringing the oil temperature up to simmering. This takes a good ten minutes or more. Place several horns in the pan five minutes or so after starting heating. These should have been prepared previously by removing any rough or dirty patches on the surface, and be reasonably clean. Smaller lengths of horn suitable for half sticks can also be immersed. Allow 15 minutes or so after simmering point is arrived at for the larger horns and 10 minutes for the smaller diameter pieces. Inspect the smaller ones after that period and if they have coloured

up satisfactorily remove from the pan. A wire grid over the pan will allow the horn to drip, then place on a rag to cool down (this can be used later for polishing shanks). Extract the larger horns after a further five minutes and treat likewise; any that look too pale can be replaced for a further period but inspect regularly. At this stage horn is extremely malleable and can be squeezed to size with channel blocks up to the heel quite readily and also shaped up along the crown and nose if you work quickly before the heat disperses. If you do any shaping up, place immediately in cold water afterwards. Do not leave any horn in the mixture as it cools down. When finally sanded down and polished the horns will show colours ranging from warm buff and ochre to various shades of amber, all richer than the original and, I feel, more attractive. The colours, generally speaking, are quite well set into the horn, not just on the surface, so should not as a rule buff out when sanding down afterwards.

For different shades again repeat the process with the other pan but add to

*Colouring ram's horn – simmering in linseed oil and dissolved shellac flakes.*

the oil/shellac mix some blue powder paint. You will need to experiment here as the blue will react with the basically orange-shaded mix to give a greenish colour. What you are aiming for is an olive shade – I find that approximately two large tablespoonfuls of the paint powder should suffice. Stir well to disperse the colour and ensure that the powder has dissolved; add more powder if the colour is not deep enough. (If the powder shade is *dark* blue you may need less.) If too light a green try more shellac flakes. When these horns are dressed down they should result in subtle shades of olive, perhaps with some suggesting a touch of blue, similar in fact to certain types of cow horn and coloured buffalo. Whatever shades result from either mix you will find that the grain structure of the horn, which is normally hardly evident, is much more visible, particularly along the outer edges of the horn.

It is best to keep the horn from contact with the base of the pan during heating to prevent scorching – I utilize the perforated loose trivet that fits into the pressure cooker. Ensure that the horns are fully covered with the oil. Odd horns with a pronounced side curl may need flattening roughly before putting in the pan otherwise part of the horn may not be covered in oil. The outcurl will slowly creep back into the horn but hopefully not before the colouring process is finished.

During the heating any blood clots in the horn (these are often fairly close to the surface) will probably erupt to form blisters. If these have not burst when the horn is removed from the pan it is often possible to push them back into place using a wooden peg or hammer handle in the vice. Usually however the bulges can be rasped and sanded clear although a shallow portion of horn will no doubt also require to be removed. You will probably find that when reheating the horn when you are shaping it up, it will work more easily than usual, this no doubt as a result of the simmering in oil.

Try to obtain a large pair of tongs for lifting the horns from the oil. Old-fashioned claw types in metal from fireside companion sets are ideal, or alternatively use wooden ones, serrating the tips as necessary to improve the grip. Ensure that any residual oil in the hollow base of any horn is poured back into the pan before removal.

Light-coloured antler can also be experimented with for colouring. I don't find the olive mix too attractive for this but the other certainly is. Times for simmering will vary of course depending upon the individual hardness of the antler so it is necessary to experiment. This also applies to horn, incidentally; harder horn from hill breeds will require a longer simmering time than softer horn.

The smell throughout the process is not too unpleasant but fairly invasive and it is advisable to utilize a garage or workshop rather than a kitchen. It also helps considerably to use a lid on the pan. I removed the rubber seals from the pressure cooker lids, also the pop-up valve; this allows a little of the smell out but hardly enough to notice. It is another matter of course once the lid is removed. If the smell is not a problem then there is no point in using the lids. Keep your nose near to the broth pot and there should be no overcooking!

# 13   Other Types of Handle Material

## RESIN HANDLES

Cast resin handles have been around for some years now and I have seen some really good ones. This of course is not too surprising when you appreciate that they are all direct copies from originals, some of which have been created by expert carvers. And if you personally are unable to carve to any decent standard, you can at least own an exact copy (colouring apart, perhaps). Even a good carver would probably not want to spend the time doing the same subject repeatedly.

There are two stages in the making of a resin handle: a) constructing the mould,

and b) casting the resin. Neither should present any great difficulties. Firstly of course you require a suitable model and, apart from the obvious sources such as an existing carving or pottery figurine, I have successfully used such unlikely objects as a pewter sitting spaniel from an ash tray, and wooden squirrel from an old decanter stopper. It is not essential for the model to have a base of the same dimensions – or shape – as the shank it is to be mounted upon as it can be easily attached to a plinth of wood or horn which can be bevelled down to fit. Size is important of course, but even a comparatively small casting can be considered for attaching to the nose of a wood or horn market stick or crook.

*Tufnol market stick.*

## THE MOULD

This is made from liquid latex rubber, which in appearance is rather like milk; painted on, it dries on the model surface and makes a flexible thin rubber skin. 'Thin' is perhaps an exaggeration in this context as I find that 15 or more coats may be required to provide a reasonable thickness. The manufacturer's instructions also state that the latex should be 'touch-dry' in 10 minutes at 20°C but in practice this was nearer an hour. Obviously this would be an extremely time-consuming process but there are two ways of circumventing this. When you obtain the latex, purchase also some 'thickener'; a few drops of this in the latex give excellent results reducing the required number of coats by at least half. Also, and this is not mentioned by the manufacturers, the 'touch-drying' stage can be reached in about one minute by lightly playing over the mould with a hair dryer or hot-air gun on low setting. Care must be exercised however not to be too close nor to dwell upon one spot, otherwise blistering will occur. Once dry, another coat can be applied immediately, and so on. It is essential that the mould is not over thin otherwise there is almost certain to be distortion when resin filled. I prefer to have them thick enough so that they hold their shape without collapsing when laid on the bench. They will also have a much longer life.

I use a half-inch (1.25cm) paintbrush with soft bristles for applying the latex but it is essential to ensure during application of the first coat in particular that brush marks are removed (just like house painting, in fact!) Also work the brush into any pockets or crevices such as ears, beaks, overlapping feathers, between toes or claws, and so on. Keep a lookout also for air bubbles, usually these will disappear with overbrushing. To ensure good detail do not use thickened latex until after three or four coats of plain latex have been applied. By the same token, ensure that the model used is clean particularly in crevices, otherwise detail in the mould will be lost as the dirt is lifted out by the latex. When dry the completed mould can be removed from the model by peeling back. Certain models may be difficult to peel but bathing in warm soapy water will normally soften the latex and facilitate removal. The mould will then of course be inside-out so roll back to normal. The manufacturers advise at this stage that the whole mould should be lightly dusted with talc to prevent the rubber sticking, particularly when stored.

## CASTING THE RESIN

For model casting you will require Filled Polyester Casting Resin, also a suitable catalyst. The resin is usually a not very attractive creamy beige colour but paint powder of any desired colour can be added. If the model is self-coloured, say for instance a black spaniel or labrador (eyes and noses excepted) then this will save painting afterwards. I also add some fine wood, antler or horn dust to the basic mix as these impart added strength. With these and any powder colour, you need to mix in thoroughly to prevent streaking and after adding the catalyst stir thoroughly, trying to eliminate any air bubbles. A suitable container for mixing would be a plastic beaker preferably with pouring lip. The exact amount of catalyst is not crucial as there is a certain amount of flexibility built into the chemical reaction but in general try to avoid adding too little. Not only will this result in a longer setting time but the mix may not set at all! Too much catalyst will have much the same effect.

Support the mould in a tray or container with about 2in (5cm) of fine sand or sieved peat. Make initially a suitable sized hole, then place the mould in it as vertically as possible. Do not allow the mould to rest on the bare bottom of the container otherwise the casting will almost certainly have a flat crown to the head.

Pour in sufficient resin to roughly half fill the mould then lift out carefully and squeeze and work it between the fingers to force out any air pockets and ensure complete penetration of the resin into all cavities. Pay particular attention to extremities and hollow parts such as ears. Then replace the mould into the tray and top up to the neck or shoulder, again trying to eliminate air bubbles. If a little resin oozes out over the sides at this stage don't worry about removing it; it will break off the mould easily after setting. The resin is of fairly thick consistency and you will find it helpful to use a small spoon or ladle or perhaps a little spatula to extract as much resin as possible from the container. The manufacturers suggest that the amount of resin required can be calculated by filling the mould with water and pouring this into a container and marking the level. In reality of course this is extremely difficult because of the vastly different consistencies of the liquids; a classic example of good theory failing to make the transition to good practice. It is sensible to have several moulds of different sizes (or capacities) handy so that any spare mixed resin can be used up. It is also possible to have a part-filled mould left standing for a while and topped up when a further mix is available. The two separate resin mixes fuse together satisfactorily.

When set (I disregard the manufacturers' times and leave overnight) peel back the latex using soapy warm water as described, if in difficulty. The base of the casting may have a sharp slightly raised rim but this will sand down flush easily enough. Any ragged edge to the latex can be trimmed straight with scissors or can be left as it will not affect any future castings. Any imperfections such as air bubble hollows or missing ear tips, and so on, can be easily repaired using an Araldite bodge with horn or wood dust. Further detailing can also be done as required, *viz.* feather or

fur markings defined or improved or added, and so on. Needle files are probably best for this but tend to clog up fairly quickly – they can be easily cleared using a small stiff brush. Small burrs with a miniature power tool are also handy.

The casting drills easily enough and shank fitting can be either by dowel or threaded rod (studding). It is in fact possible to fit a length of studding in position before the resin sets in the mould but this needs careful timing. If inserted too early the studding will not stay vertical and naturally if the resin has set too firmly it is not possible to push it into position.

If the latex of the mould is fairly thick it is possible to make quite a good number of castings from it, but ensure when it is unrolled each time after removing from the casting that the inside of the latex is clean. You may occasionally have to remove small particles of resin from the mould interior as these would naturally cause blemishes in any further castings. You may cause small tears in the latex from time to time and these also would cause blemishes on any future use. If not too large it is an easy matter to effect a repair to any tear by painting over the spot with several coats of thickened latex (on the *outside* of the mould, of course!).

Acrylics are probably best for painting your finished casting as watercolours would require several coats to cover the base shade, and oils usually take far too long to dry. Inks in general are not very satisfactory as the surface is not really porous enough for them to be effective. Protect painted castings with several coats of varnish.

If the eyes are not very satisfactorily shaped, glass, wood or horn ones can of course be inserted in the usual way. Resin heads, because of their base colours, will often look particularly unlifelike initially – but try painting eyes in first to introduce some animation (the 'real' ones can be inserted later).

Apart from the plain filled casting resin described there are other variations in finish available, *viz.* coloured veined marble effect; imitation ivory; metal (bronze, and so on); also staining and antiquing. Any good model shop should be able to advise about these finishes and also provide the relevant materials. I would think that the metal finish could possibly give some good results although the process is more complicated than ordinary resin casting. This involves painting all over on the inside of the mould with a lacquer, then allowing it to dry. The metal, which is in a coarse powdered form, is mixed with more lacquer and a further coat applied. This bonds to the first coat. The mould is then turned the right way round (that is, lacquered part inside) and resin filled in the usual way. When set, the casting is lightly burnished with steel wool and the fur or feather texturing, for instance, is highlighted. This would be particularly impressive in a model of a golden eagle for instance, also perhaps an otter. Whether it is a viable proposition in view of the expense and the complications in casting is a moot point, especially as rather similar effects could be achieved by careful colouring with some of the various textured paints available. Neither would you have the problem of metal textured eyeballs to contend with . . .

## TUFNOL

This man-made material has been around for more than sixty years but has had infrequent use as stick handle material

during that period. There is no doubt that it would have enjoyed greater popularity had it been better known and perhaps more readily available. It is very aptly named, being virtually unbreakable, certainly unwearoutable, and resists cracks, splits or even dents. Its only fault really is in the rather limited colours, ranging loosely from pale cream to a deep brown, whilst black is also available. It is known in the trade as resin-impregnated fabric laminate; the weave of the cotton fabric in its construction varies and will normally look rather similar to grain in wood or some kinds of horn on a finished piece. Various uses in industry include electric insulating boards, silent running gear, cogs and bearings, washers and bushes, also rods and tubes.

Most of the pieces that I have obtained have been in mid to darker brown shades. The lighter colour is quite nice but the latter does not appeal at all. I tried to lighten the colour with household bleach but this had no effect, even when undiluted. It can however be left under glass (after shaping and finishing) on a shelf in a porch, conservatory or greenhouse for instance and should lighten up considerably over a period. Summer is obviously the best time to try this experiment and the piece must naturally be turned over periodically. Do not expect quick results as the colour is very fast.

Any pieces obtained will usually be flat-sided in boards or blocks and this will facilitate the drawing of a handle pattern. Cutting out is much slower than with timber and if a hand saw is used the manufacturers recommend a coarse hacksaw, but circular or bandsaws are obviously preferable, if available. If using handsaw or bandsaw it is much easier to chain drill around the handle outline first (see under

'Block Sticks'). The roughed-out hand-piece can be worked easily enough with rasps or engineer's files or a good tool steel scraper, also of course with power tools. Any abrasives used will soon become dust-clogged but can be cleared easily enough by tapping or by brass wire brush. Sanding down in general is a very dusty procedure and a face mask is virtually obligatory. If the material is to be carved I would advise against the use of gouges, and so on, as these will very soon lose their edge. Burrs in a power tool, preferably with a flexi shaft, are a much better proposition.

All grades of Tufnol take a very fine finish, comparable to any wood or horn. Linseed oil gives particularly good results but the material will respond readily to any polishing agent. The black type usually will not show any 'grain' and when polished has the rather unnatural look of plastic, but there again so does black buffalo horn! I do not care for the plain type of handle in this colour but superb dog heads such as Labrador and Cocker Spaniel can be created, also Cormorant, Tufted Duck, and with grey and white additions, an excellent Badger. The feel of a finished handle is similar to horn – perhaps a mite cold on a winter's day – but it will soon warm up. The weight is roughly comparable with that of horn, perhaps slightly heavier by an ounce or so in a crook handle, but not enough to un-balance a stick.

In general this is hardly the sort of material that can be purchased over the counter from the manufacturers as it is made for industry. However, there is invariably a good selection of offcuts available through trade sources and these will normally be trimmed to your needs on request. They will also be reasonably priced.

As a stickmaking material Tufnol does not appeal to everyone obviously but for an everyday hard-wearing, knockabout sort of stick it cannot be beaten.

## DEER FOOT HANDLES

I have never been able to understand why certain stickmakers, albeit a small minority, have a mild compulsion to make deer foot handle sticks. The whole idea of mounting an animal's foot as a handle is bizarre to say the least. And why deer in particular? Why not sheep or goat, for instance, as this would be equally logical? For that matter, why not some sort of handle from horse or cow hooves? They at least are horn. Certainly nobody could claim that deer foot handles are comfortable in the hand. The fur runs one way only for a start, and is stretched tightly

*Pair roe deer feet thumbsticks. Thumb saddles in buffalo horn and purple heart.*

over bone; not a very pleasant feeling grip at all. And that is when dry; when wet it is unspeakable. Furthermore, if you use one at all regularly, you will find that the handle is reduced to no more than skin and bone with a few shreds of fur lingering here and there. Such an unpleasant handle hardly bears thinking about.

My advice would be to resist any temptation to make one.

# 14  Jointing and Finish

The two commonest ways of jointing handle to shank are by studding or dowel. Studding is mild steel-threaded rod and the diameter commonly used is ¼in–⅜in (0.6–1cm). Holes are drilled in both handle and shank and studding lengths up to 5in (12.5cm) or 6in (15cm) are usually recommended. It is an easy enough task to drill a vertical hole in a handle held vertically in a vice, but infinitely more difficult to repeat this in a 4ft (1.2m) long shank. The slightest divergence from the vertical results in difficulties in lining up the faces of the joint. Drilling out a shank too means that a theoretical weak spot has been introduced at a spot where one can expect a fair amount of lateral movement whenever the stick is used. And in all fairness to whichever type of adhesive is used, a glued joint containing metal never has great strength due to its non-porous nature. All in all, studding makes an inferior joint for a working stick, unless strengthened by a collar.

The dowel method is basically simple and gives a stronger joint – it *is* used in furniture-making after all! Drill a suitable hole, usually ½in (1.25cm) to ¾in (2cm) in diameter, depending on shank dimensions, to a depth of about 1in (2.5cm) or so in the handle. It is a popular fallacy that a longer dowel will result in a stronger joint. Measure the depth of the drilled hole and mark the top of the shank correspondingly. Circle the stick from this point using either a sharp knife or coping saw, cutting through the bark but not too deeply into the wood. Hold the stick under one arm (or rest along the vice jaws or workbench if you prefer) and bring the blade of a sharp knife – preferably with a reasonably fine blade – back into the cut portion and take off the bark together with a thin sliver of wood towards the stick end. Repeat around the stick, then looking along the stick from this end, trim back towards you, rounding up neatly as you go. You will see

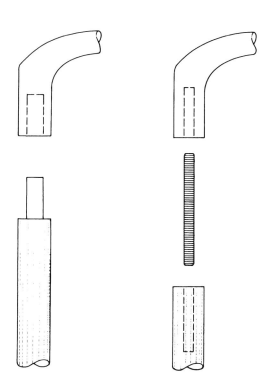

*Two types of joint. L. dowel on end of shank. This makes the strongest joint. R. drilling both handle and shank to joint with threaded metal rod.*

111

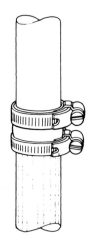
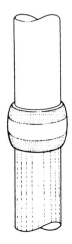

*Fitting a horn collar over a joint: (L to R) heated horn held in position by Jubilee clips at top and bottom; Jubilee clips removed show pressure marks on horn; horn dressed down and polished.*

that the dowel is now cone-shaped, narrowing towards the trimmed end. Make the dowel parallel-sided by carefully cutting back towards the cut line to form a shoulder. Try for handle fit and repeat the trimming stages until a 'twist-fit' is reached. If the handle can be 'push-fitted' fairly easily the dowel has been trimmed too far.

Twist the handle around until it is seating neatly – there is always one spot better than anywhere else. If satisfied that the joint faces are well-fitted, run a pencil mark down from the handle on to the top of the shank. Remove the handle and score the dowel lengthways, but not too deeply, with a knife point or fine gouge. This allows any build-up of glue to escape towards the joint rather than forming a cushion at the end of the dowel and possibly upsetting the firm fit of the handle. Now glue up the dowel, twist into place lining up the pencil marks, and leave to set after removing any surplus glue around the joint.

A collar adds strength and looks to a joint, the best ones being of horn or well-marked antler. Antler must be a fairly

exact fit and you can spend a tedious few minutes filing out a drilled piece before it may be acceptable. Horn is often tapering along, say, its 1in (2.5cm) or so length (particularly cow horn) so it must first be heated, then a tapered peg of the desired dimensions hammered in the narrower end until both top and bottom diameters are near similar. Slip over the joint after gluing and fix Jubilee clips tightly over the top and bottom of the collar. Heat the collar all round and tighten the clips as the horn softens. Leave to set, then remove clips. The marks left by the clips are sanded down or filed and the collar is best made up into the barrel shape. Final tidying up and polishing can be done at the same time as the handle.

After cleaning up the shank and handle put the finishing touches to the stick. The handle must be as smooth as possible – antler apart of course – with no scratches evident. Various grades of emery cloth and 'wet and dry' abrasives are used and lengths of 'strapping' are useful, that is, strips of emery cloth used in a pulled to-and-fro motion. I find that the most time-consuming material to work upon is black buffalo, where myriad hair-line scratches seem to be virtually irremovable. Usually I cut the corner here towards the finish by using black wax shoe polish, either in conjunction with a little water or brazed on with a hot-air gun or hair dryer. The horn burnishes beautifully afterwards! Use linseed oil on wood handles and repeat the application until the surface remains tacky. Regular buffing with a soft cloth, and further applications as necessary, will result in a very pleasing finish. The oil can also be used on antler handles, as can car-rubbing compound (either liquid or paste) or brass polish, both of which are used extensively for bringing up the lustre on horn.

Varnish has its devotees for finish on a stick but although initially attractive the fine lustre soon becomes untidy in use. Then it is a question of rubbing down and re-varnishing. Linseed does not have these problems, neither is there a need to clean brushes afterwards – nor is any wasted as a skin does not appear on the liquid once it has been used!

# Appendix

## A FEW TIPS

1. However carefully you handle black-thorn or hawthorn when stick cutting, even wearing thornproof gloves, you will nonetheless almost certainly at some time get a thorn embedded in your hand or wrist. These can be difficult to remove, especially if you are a mite squeamish in excavating with a needle. But there is a much better remedy. Put some soft soap on the pad of a piece of sticking plaster. Sprinkle over a small amount of brown sugar, place in position and stick down firmly. Remove the following morning and the splinter should be found lying on the lint.

2. The standard epoxy glue comes in a twin pack: adhesive and hardener. Naturally when mixing you use (or try to) equal quantities from each tube. Nonetheless you will nearly always be left with some surplus in one or other of the tubes. As the adhesive normally has a built-in margin of flexibility in the mixing amounts, no harm should have been done. To save this imbalance some manufacturers now offer a package where the twin tubes are more rigid and brazed together. Adhesive and hardener are squeezed out simultaneously by a twin plunger arrangement which appears to solve the problem. In practice however the plunger is of not-very-rigid polythene or similar material and pressure is usually applied unevenly, squeezing out more from one tube than the other! No improvement in fact. If you look at the tubes you will see that (invariably) they are of smaller size than the standard pack, and they cost more. So you pay more, receive less, and there is still no certainty of an equal mix.

3. Don't return from a walk, then place your favourite horn head stick near a heat source, whether chimney breast, radiator or whatever. This will cause your handle to revert, however slightly, to the original horn shape, undoing the work in fashioning. I knew one Dales farmer who habitually propped his crook against the barn wall. The stick was accidentally

*Banksia nut knob stick.*

114

knocked over and the handle ended up on top of a fermenting manure heap, distorting the 'horn heid' considerably!

4. The banksia nut comes from a Western Australian hardwood tree and takes seven years to mature, I understand. It is quite a heavyweight, usually 5in to 6in (12.5cm to 15cm) long with one end tapering and the other rounded. Diameter can be up to 4in (10cm) or so. The nut is characterized by being honeycombed with deep oval-shaped holes ⅜in to ½in (1cm to 1.25cm) wide and the centre of the nut is solid wood. Cut in two, one half of a nut can be shaped into an unusual knob stick handle and can be shanked by a dowel, usually from the tapered end after trimming to fit. They are available from many exotic timber suppliers, also craft outlets, and so on, and are popular with turners for fashioning table-lamp bases. The cost, sold individually, is usually around £2.00. Try to obtain one with fairly evenly spaced honey-combing and remove any seeds remaining in the holes after shaping up. The nut sands down to a good finish and will polish up using either varnish or linseed. It's a rich dark brown in colour.

5. It is rather annoying to find that the part translucent characteristic of horn after polishing results in the light colour of the dowel showing through the base of a handle after shanking. This can be disguised easily enough in black buffalo horn by staining the dowel black, but you will need to experiment with the colour when other horn is involved. Use stain, needless to say, or watercolour, but not paint, which could weaken the strength of the glued joint, and ensure that the dowel

is dry before applying the adhesive.

6. Save wood, antler and horn dust from your workshop for using in 'bodge' mixes for disguising irregularities. Mixed with adhesive they can cosmetically improve and occasionally hide completely any cracks, hollows, holes and other imperfections. Shavings too can be useful in plugging the hollow base of horn handles before the final dowelling. One or two shades of powder paint can also come in useful (black in particular) as can Tufnol dust. I store mine in small pill bottles or 35mm cassette holders and label them according to colour and whether fine or coarse. Even fine dust from alloy or brass and copper has its uses on occasion.

*Boxed set of miniature horn handle sticks (4½in (11.5cm)).*

7. If you want to try your luck at shows don't put your sticks in 'pre-entry' ones. These are organized purely to ensure that none but local competitors known to the show organisers are the winners. You will be assured success however if you are friendly with or related to the Judge, or if you will be judging at a future show where he himself will be entering sticks. This is known as Backscratching, a phenomenon widespread in any type of show where there is a competitive element . . .

8. Miniature sticks are not 'real' sticks, of course, but scale models of the real thing. Following my suggestion some years ago, classes for sets of five miniature sticks can be seen at many stick shows, usually attracting considerable attention.

   The criteria used are simple but flexible – sticks must not be longer than nine inches overall, may be made of any material and may be mounted on the maker's choice of base. Needless to say, they should be to scale.

The most eye-catching are invariably those with horn heads, although I have seen bone used occasionally. I also feel that the best presentations are mounted on a simple base of polished wood, including burr, antler length or coronet, or a piece of suitable horn. Some stickmakers, however, prefer a fancy setting; I have seen carved representations of a shepherd complete with collie and various combinations of sheep and lambs; a leaping trout; a full-size crook handle; and a right-angled sheep hurdle with sticks propped up. In these instances, unfortunately, the judges often appear to be swayed by the setting rather than the stick. I suppose that two classes, one for a plain base with the other for fancy, would be the solution but entries would possibly not justify this.

The simplest horn handles can be made from offcuts or pressed sheets of horn, and the shanks in various ways. I made mine from bamboo chop sticks, for instance!

# Useful Addresses

## STICKMAKERS' ASSOCIATIONS

*South Wales Stickmakers*
*Sec.* S.G. Hadley, 59, Fonmon Park Road, Rhoose, CF62 3BG

*Midland Counties Stickmakers*

Sec. J. Musialowski,. 1 Harris Drive, Newton, Hyde, Cheshire, SK14 4UB

*Northern Stickmakers*

*Sec.* A. Robson, Brunstock, West High Horse Close, Rowlands Gill, Co. Durham
*Quarterly Magazine*

*Scottish Crookmakers Society*

*Sec.* Mrs. D. M. Hope, 9, Caulside, Canonbie, Dumfries

## GENERAL STICKMAKING COMPONENTS

*Denmar Supplies*
Walford Lodge, Walford, Baschurch, Shrewsbury, SY4 2HL

*D.W. Davies*
Y Ddol, Llandewi Brefi, Tregaron, Dyfed, SY25 6RS

*B. Bannister*
Stone House, Cowgill, Dent, Cumbria, LA10 5RL

## BOOKS ON STICKMAKING

*Conch-Y-Bonddu Books*
Papyrus, Pentrehedyn Street, Machynlleth, Powys, SY20 8DJ

## FERRULES

*Stroud Metal Co. Ltd.*
Dudbridge, Stroud, Gloucestershire, GL5 3EZ

## GLASS EYES

*Lorne Taxidermy*
Kilnhillock Cottage, By Cullen, Buckie, Banffshire, AB56 2TB

*Pintail Carvings*
20, Sheppenhall Grove, Aston, Nantwich, Cheshire, CW5 8DF

*Snowdonia Taxidermy*
Llanrwst, Conwy, LL26 0HU (Urethane Elastomer liquid for casting also stocked)

# EXOTIC TIMBER; BURRS, ETC.

*John Boddy Ltd.*
Riverside Sawmills, Boroughbridge,
N. Yorkshire, YO5 9LJ

*Craft Supplies Ltd.*
The Mill, Millersdale, Buxton, Derbyshire,
SK17 8SN

*Wood Products*
25, Bradley Road, West Wylam, NE42 5EG
Burrs a speciality. Stick handles to order.

*Keenleysides Ltd.*
Bedlington Station, Bedlington,
Northumberland

# KNIVES FOR CARVING

*Barry Scott*
2 Seaton Crescent, Holywell, Tyne &
Wear, NE2S 0LF

# TUFNOL

*Tufnol Ltd.*
PO Box 376, Well Head Lane, Perry Barr,
Birmingham, B42 2TB

# BUFFALO HORN

*Hillend Horncraft*
85, Hillend Road, Clarkston, Glasgow, G76
7XT

# RAM'S HORN

*Lesley Parkin*
Hermitage School House, Via Hawick,
Roxburghshire, TD9 0LX

# REINDEER ANTLER

Reindeer House, Glenmore, Via
Aviemore, Inverness-shire

# NOTE

*Red Deer antler* is generally available in
spring from most Scottish Highland
estates. Contact the estate stalker in each
case (local enquiries are usually fruitful).

# Further Reading

Dike, C., *Walking Sticks* (Shire Publications, 1995)

Douglas, J. M., *Blackthorn Lore and the Art of Making Walking Sticks* (Alloway Publishing, 1984)

Fossel, T., *Walking & Working Sticks* (The Apostle Press, 1986)

Gowan, L., *The Craft of Stickmaking* (The Crowood Press, 1991)

Grant, D. & Hart, E., *Shepherd's Crooks & Walking Sticks* (Dalesman Books, 1976; revised edition 1985)

Griff Jones, R. & Owen, M., *Collen, Cyllel a Chorn* (Carreg Gwalch, 1995, in Welsh)

Griff Jones, R. & Owen, M., *Ways with Hazel and Horn* (Carreg Gwalch, 1996)

Griffin, R., *Wooden Tops* (Privately published in 1996; available from 47 Leighton Road, Uttoxeter, ST14 8BL)

Hart, E., *Walking Sticks* (The Crowood Press, 1986)

Tulip, N., *The Art of Stick Dressing* (Frank Graham, 1978)

Wolfe, T., *Carving Canes & Walking Sticks* (Schiffer Publishing Company, USA, 1994)

# Index

abrasives   11, 12, 13, 37, 112
acrylic   31, 33, 87, 89, 107
alder   19
ash   16, 17, 24, 26, 38, 88, 90

balance   14, 21, 22, 109
bending
   horn   62, 64, 67, 78, 74
   wood   21, 22, 25, 26
billy goat horn   65–66, 79, 95
blackthorn   15, 17, 18, 20, 24, 40, 43, 56, 114
block sticks   34–38, 41, 81
bodge   37, 73, 89, 90, 97, 107
buffalo horn   79, 95
   black 66–67, 79, 81, 88, 92, 95, 109, 113, 115
   coloured   68, 79
burr   39, 40

carving (*see also* fancy sticks)   11, 12, 26–34, 52–55, 84–94
channel blocks   70, 72, 73
checks (splits)   17, 18, 36
cherry   15, 20
clamps   *see* 'channel blocks'
collars   41, 42, 43, 56, 95, 97, 112
cow horn   63–64, 79, 81, 95, 112
crooks   30–31, 37, 51, 59, 63, 71, 74, 84, 86
crown   26, 29, 36, 37, 43, 62, 71, 73, 74, 85, 86, 106

deer antler   42, 43, 44, 42–57, 81, 83, 98, 99, 103, 112, 113, 115
deer feet   109, 110

dolly (cylinder)   70, 71, 73, 74
dowel   32, 42, 48, 49, 56, 97, 98, 100, 107, 111, 115

elm   40

fancy sticks (*see also* carving)   11, 23, 26–34, 38, 52–55, 84–94, 99, 100, 109
finish   13, 34, 67, 112–113
flat-fit drills   11, 56
foreign timbers (exotics)   38, 39, 40
formers   71, 73, 74

glue   42, 47, 82, 89, 90, 92, 97, 114
grafting wax   17, 34
grain   17, 19, 36, 37, 38, 44, 67

half head   30, 38, 86–90
half stick   30, 31, 81–83, 102
hawthorn   20, 114
hazel   14, 16, 18, 23, 24, 33, 37, 38, 56
holly   15, 18, 19, 20, 24, 33, 37, 56
honeysuckle 'twist'   24, 31, 42, 43
hot-air gun   11, 17, 21, 37, 42, 52, 72, 56, 81

inks (colouring/staining)   19, 32, 33, 34, 38, 87, 88, 93

jersey cabbage stick   25
joints   41, 42, 43, 55, 97, 111–112
juniper   40

knives   9, 18, 111
knob sticks   23, 26, 30, 31, 38, 95, 115
knots   13, 16, 17, 19, 20, 31, 37

laburnum   40
laurel   40
leg crook   71, 74
length   14, 15, 16, 17, 23, 24, 25, 47
linseed oil   16, 34, 37, 38, 57, 64, 72, 78,
    109, 113, 115

market stick   30, 37, 38, 59, 63, 71, 74, 84,
    86
microwave   42, 62, 77–80
mountain ash (rowan)   15

neck 29, 41, 70, 74, 86
nose   31, 36, 37, 38, 71, 74

painting   31, 33, 51, 53, 87–90, 93, 94, 115
pyrography   12, 88, 89, 92, 100

ramscurl   63, 74, 75, 91
ram's horn   60–63, 64, 66, 67, 68, 69–75,
    79, 84, 91, 97, 99, 101
resin   105–108
root   15, 24
rosewood   38

sash cramp   71, 74, 75
saws   9, 10, 11
seasoning
    wood   15, 16, 34
    horn   62

shows   17, 84, 85, 86, 88, 90, 91, 116
spruce   19
squeezing up ('rounding up')   71, 73,
    78
stains   17, 18, 19, 20, 37, 57, 101–104
    coffee   18, 19, 20, 37, 57
    permanganate of potash   20, 57
steel wool 13, 16, 18, 19, 20, 21
storage   16
straightening   21–22
strapping   13, 37
studding   82, 97, 98, 99, 107, 111

taper   16, 17, 18, 20, 23, 36, 62, 65, 73, 74,
    75
thumbsticks   23–24, 38, 41, 42, 46, 50,
    95–100
tools   9–13
tufnol   95, 108, 109, 115

varnish   19, 33, 34, 54, 94, 100, 113
vices   9, 10, 21, 34, 36, 37, 70, 71–75, 81,
    82, 83, 93, 95, 98, 99

walnut   40
whistle stick handle   48, 49
workshop   13

yew   19, 40